Children's Rights and Participation in Residential Care

Carolyne Willow
Children's Residential Care Unit
National Children's Bureau

The National Children's Bureau was established as a registered charity in 1963. Our purpose is to identify and promote the interests of all children and young people and to improve their status in a diverse society.

We work closely with professionals and policy makers to improve the lives of all children but especially young children under five, those affected by family instability, children with special needs or disabilities and those suffering the effects of poverty and deprivation.

We collect and disseminate information about children and promote good practice in children's services through research, policy and practice development, publications, seminars, training and an extensive library and information service.

The Bureau works in partnership with Children in Scotland and Children in Wales.

The views expressed in this book are those of the author and not necessarily those of the National Children's Bureau.

ISBN 1 874579 92 X

Published by National Children's Bureau Enterprises Ltd, 8 Wakley Street, London, EC1V 7QE

National Children's Bureau Enterprises is the trading company for the National Children's Bureau (Registered Charity number 258825).

Typeset by Books Unlimited (Nottm), NG19 7QZ

Printed by Redwood Books Ltd.

Contents

List of tables

Acknowledgements

Many people have helped me prepare this book. My special thanks goes to: all the young people who were involved in the *Children's Rights* and *Participation in the Care Environment* Project; staff and managers, from Birmingham's residential homes, who commented on the draft; Barbara Hearn, Rachel Hodgkin, Ruth Sinclair and Phil Youdan at the National Children's Bureau; David Berridge; Gerison Lansdown; Linda Marshall; and Jenny Morris. I am very grateful to the young people who entered the book cover competition, especially to Stephanie Ensor whose winning entry appears on the front cover. Finally, thanks to Barbara Kahan whose help and encouragement have been invaluable.

The author

Since graduating in applied social studies in 1988, Carolyne Willow has worked as a child care social worker in Nottinghamshire and lectured in social policy. She has also been a welfare rights officer. Prior to joining the National Children's Bureau, Carolyne was Leicestershire's Children's Rights Officer. She is currently chairperson of Children's Rights Officers and Advocates, a national organisation of children's rights professionals.

Chapter one
Introduction

We were brought up in care, and we know what we missed – the every-day, taken-for-granted things: people to call Mum and Dad; being together as a family through pleasure and adversity; watching each other grow up; family photographs ... not photographs of groups in children's homes. We hated categorization. We were just children, and we wanted fun and love. We wanted to grow up as normal kids ... We wanted to have birthday parties, to invite friends who would come to our house. We longed to be accepted.

(Tom O'Neill talking about his experiences of care during the 1940s in *A Place Called Hope* 1981, p.81*)*

This book aims to help residential social workers promote the rights and participation of young people in residential homes owned and managed by local authorities and private and voluntary organisations. While it is anticipated that residential social workers will make up the main read-ership, the intention has been to produce a text which will benefit a range of professionals directly involved in providing services to young people who live in residential care: teachers; field social workers; health visi-tors, school nurses and community paeditricians; youth workers; and children's rights officers and advocates. It should also prove helpful to inspectors and to those who have the main responsibility for planning and evaluating local authority social services.

During the preparation of this book, there was great temptation to make it an accessible resource for young people too. Finally, it was decided that the book should be primarily geared to the needs of staff. Rights-based information and literature exclusively written for (and often by) young people who are looked after, is increasing all the time. Conversely, there is a conspicuous lack of accessible rights-based literature for the adults who have so much power over these young people's lives.

Busy practitioners do not have much time to search for, and read, texts which carefully and calmly explore the nature of childhood, and the rights of young people: it is therefore not surprising that social work discussions about children's rights often seem to be largely informed by fear and misunderstanding. The results can be extremely worrying. Within residential care, for example, it is common for discussions about respect, dignity and rights to be seen as secondary matters to issues such as control, restraint and violence towards staff. While these subjects are very important they should not eclipse fundamental questions about how *young people* should be treated in residential settings.

The idea for this book originated from the author's work with young people and staff in residential homes while managing a National Children's Bureau project. The children's rights and participation in the care environment project was established in September 1994 for two years. Based in the West Midlands, the aims of the project were:

- to examine and develop residential environments which recognise and enhance the rights of young people;

- to encourage the active participation of young people in their own care plans and in the running and development of their establishments.

The primary focus of the project was in-depth development work with six community homes in Birmingham, Coventry and Sandwell: one of these homes offers pre-adoption and fostering care for children under 12 years; another provides short-term care to disabled young people; two offer emergency and medium-stay care for adolescents; one is a community home for young men; and the sixth is a long-stay home for those over 12 years. The project also undertook work with young people living in 12 different community homes in the West Midlands and with parents of disabled young people.

During the summer of 1994, residential staff in over 35 homes in the West Midlands were sent draft copies of this book to establish if they would find a document like this useful. Approximately 25 per cent of staff replied, each giving comprehensive feedback. Their responses were extremely heartening. Not only did they show that a book of this nature was much needed, they also illustrated that there are many people working in residential care who have a genuine commitment to the notion, and everyday practice, of children's rights.

Throughout the course of the project many young people gave invaluable information on their experiences in residential and foster care, and their ideas for improving services. They expressed their views through play, interviews, drawing, writing, talking, drama and poems. While young people were not directly involved in preparing this book, their influence was significant. Throughout the project's work we continually stressed that by listening to young people we could ensure that staff development was firmly grounded in young people's experiences.

The book is divided into ten chapters:

- **Chapter one: Introduction**.
- **Chapter two: Children's residential care: an overview**
  Examines the role and purpose of residential care.
- **Chapter three: History and development of children's residential care**
  Outlines developments in the use and purpose of residential care, particularly in the shift towards viewing young people who live in residential care as people with rights.
- **Chapter four: Children's rights in residential care**
  Describes the historical role of young people in changing and improving residential services. Provides a comprehensive summary of independent organisations and individuals available to young people.
- **Chapter five: The United Nations Convention on the Rights of the Child**
  Highlights Articles which are most relevant to young people living in residential care and suggests ways of implementing the Convention in residential settings.
- **Chapter six: The Children Act 1989**
  Summarises the key features of the Children Act 1989 in relation to young people's rights in residential care.
- **Chapter seven: Guidance and regulations**
  Outlines young people's entitlements and the responsibilities of local authorities.
- **Chapter eight: Children's rights: current issues and concerns**
  Explores topical debates in children's rights and challenges popular myths.
- **Chapter nine: Participation in residential care**
  Discusses the benefits of, and obstacles to, participation. Provides many practical examples where participation can be encouraged in residential care.
- **Chapter ten: Conclusion**.

Terminology

There is no true definition of a child. Childhood is socially constructed and conceptions of what a is child change over time (Aries 1962; Hoyles 1989; Rogers 1992). As a consequence, legislation is inconsistent and gives mixed messages about the age at which children acquire different responsibilities and adult status. Experience tells us that there is no clear point in human development where young people enter adulthood.

The Children Act 1989 mainly applies to people up to the age of 18 years while the United Nations Convention relates exclusively to people up to the age of 18 years.

For simplicity, throughout this book the term 'young people' is used to refer to *all* people who are under 18 years. Occasionally the term 'children' is used to loosely refer to people under 12 years. The term 'children's rights' refers to a concept and is not descriptive.

Using this book

The primary purpose of this book is to stimulate informed debate, help raise awareness and develop practical methods of promoting young people's rights and participation in residential settings. Exercises are included throughout; these can be completed by individuals and staff teams. Those which are intended for completion may be photocopied. The book should therefore prove useful in: staff induction; supervision; staff meetings; staff training and development; and discussions between staff and young people.

Chapter two
Children's residential care: an overview

Residential care is where people live in groups away from their families.

Barbara Kahan in her book, *Growing Up in Groups* (1994, pp.11-12), estimated that over 150,000 young people in England and Wales lived in groups away from their families and local communities in 1992. This approximate figure increases to 200,000 when we add the number of disabled young people living in residential care (Russell cited in Morris 1995, p.39).

The types of residential care which Kahan included in her comprehensive analysis are: residential care provided by local authorities and voluntary child care organisations; boarding schools; private children's homes; secure units; youth treatment centres and penal institutions; and hospitals.

By comparing the number of young people living in group environments with the general population of people aged under 18 (OPCS, 1994) we can calculate that approximately one in every 60 young people lives in some form of residential care.

At 31 March 1995, 49,000 young people were looked after by local authorities in England (Department of Health, 1996). The majority – 65 per cent – were looked after by foster carers. This reflects a growing trend away from placing young people in local authority residential care toward family placements. Statistics from previous decades reveal a reversal in the use of foster and residential care; in 1946, for example, 71 per cent of young people in care were accommodated in residential homes (Packman 1981, p.26). This period was before the modern child care service was established by the Children Act 1948. There is a growing belief that there exists a fostering saturation point above which demand for placements exceeds supply. It is unlikely therefore that the current percentage of young people in foster placements will increase much higher – indeed, the actual numbers of young people in foster care has not significantly increased since the early 1970s.

In 1991 the Department of Health issued clear guidance to local authorities in relation to residential child care. The introduction to this guidance summarised changes in the use of residential care.

> *Whilst residential solutions are used less frequently overall, the young people in the homes are older than before, and older than other young people in care. Placements are frequently of short duration and some are made at critical times when other arrangements are changing or have broken down.... Children's homes are provided for a range of purposes: some are a long-term base for a child growing up; others provide accommodation for a period while specific tasks are achieved. Some of the children have suffered the most distressing life experiences and working with them calls for skills of the highest order.*

(Department of Health 1991, p.1)

Within local authorities residential provision for young people encompasses:

- community homes
- community homes with education
- secure accommodation
- hostels.

Other forms of residential provision for young people who are looked after – therapeutic communities and refuges or safe houses for runaways – are mostly provided by private and voluntary organisations.

Young people live in these different types of residential homes for varying periods of time – homes will normally be classified as short, medium or long stay. Most local authorities have separate community homes offering short- or long-term care to disabled young people and their families. Occasionally local authorities have homes for young women or young men only and others will have homes for mixed age groups. Many local authorities have a policy of not admitting children under the age of 12 years to residential care, although in practice this is occasionally adapted to allow siblings to be placed together. While a number of private and commercial organisations have opened homes specialising in the care of black young people, to date no local authority has established a black-led home for young people (Jones and others, 1992).

Every residential home is required to have a Statement of Purpose and Function (see tables 1 and 2, pp. 8-9). This Statement gives important information including details about the young people and staff who live and work in the home (Part 1 Schedule 1 of Children's Homes Regulations 1991).

Residential care is part of a package of support services provided to children and families by local authorities. While most people working in local authorities know the names of different residential homes, or day nurseries and family centres, precise knowledge about these services is often lacking. Departmental reorganisations, home closures and changes in purpose and function all hinder maintaining up-to-date information. Some larger local authorities have a large stock of residential homes while others have relatively few or none: Birmingham, for example, currently has 31 local authority community homes compared to Sandwell's two and none in Warwickshire.

Local authorities with fewer residential homes do not necessarily use residential services less frequently; they instead often purchase services from other local authorities, voluntary organisations and the growing private sector.

Where there is insufficient residential accommodation locally it is not uncommon for Statements of Purpose and Function to be breached, to the detriment of young people and staff.

All private sector homes which provide care and accommodation for more than three young people must be registered under Part VIII of the Children Act 1989. **Young people who are looked after in residential care have the same legal entitlements irrespective of whether the home they live in is managed and owned by a local authority, or a private or voluntary organisation.**

Table 1: Statement of Purpose and Function, as required by the Children's Homes Regulations 1991

Statement to be kept relating to children's homes

Part 1 (Particulars to be included in statement)

1. The purpose for which the children's home is established, and the objectives to be attained with regard to children accommodated in the home.

2. The name and address of the responsible body, and of the person in charge of the children's home if different.

3. The following details about the children for whom it is intended that accommodation should be provided:
   a) their age range;
   b) their sex;
   c) the number of children;
   d) whether children are selected by reference to criteria other than age or sex, and, if so, those criteria.

4. The organisational structure of the children's home.

5. The experience of the person in charge of the children's home, the staff and others working there, and details of qualifications held by any of those persons relevant to their work in the home, or to the care of children.

6. The facilities and services to be provided within the children's home for the children accommodated there.

7. The arrangements made to protect and promote the health of the children accommodated there.

8. The fire precautions and associated emergency procedures.

9. The arrangements made for religious observance by any child accommodated there.

10. The arrangements made for contact between a child accommodated there and his parents, any person who is not a parent of his but who has parental responsibility for him, relatives and friends.

11. The methods of control and discipline and the disciplinary measures used there, the circumstances in which any measures will be used and who will be permitted to authorise them.

12. The procedure for dealing with any unauthorised absence of a child from the home.

13. The arrangements for dealing with any representation (including any complaint).

14. The arrangements for the education of any child accommodated there.

15. The arrangements for dealing with reviews under section 26 of the cases of every child accommodated there.

Table 2: Statement of Purpose and Function, as required by the Children's Homes Regulations 1991

Statement to be kept relating to children's homes

Part 2 (Persons to whom statement is to be made available for inspection)

1. The person in charge of the children's home.

2. The staff of the children's home and any other persons working there.

3. The children accommodated in the children's home.

4. The parent of any child accommodated in the children's home.

5. Any person who is not a parent of a child accommodated in the children's home, but who has parental responsibility for such a child.

6. Any local authority looking after or having the care of a child accommodated in the children's home where they are not responsible for the management of the home.

7. Any voluntary organisation providing accommodation for a child accommodated in the children's home where they are not responsible for the management of the home.

8. Any local education authority which has placed a child in the children's home or is considering doing so.

Young people who are looked after: the law

Since the implementation of the Children Act in October 1991, young people who are looked after by local authorities are either accommodated, in care or detained. These terms are described below.

Accommodated

Accommodated (Section 20, Children Act 1989) means that the local authority is providing the young person with accommodation and will look after that young person in partnership with her/his parents (or anyone else with parental responsibility). The local authority does not have parental powers. Parents of young people who are accommodated can ask for their child to return home at any time. The local authority cannot prevent this unless it seeks a court order where staff must demonstrate that the young person is likely to suffer significant harm if she/he is not looked after by the local authority.

Young people who are 16 years or over can ask to be accommodated by local authorities without the agreement or consent of their parents. Those who are accommodated can request to leave the care of the local authority once they reach 16; parental agreement is not required. This does not, however, mean that young people who are accommodated by local authorities *must* leave residential care on or soon after their sixteenth birthday; they can be accommodated in community homes until their twenty-first birthday (Section 20(5), Children Act 1989), although this is extremely rare. It is important that pressure of accommodation does not cause young people to be evicted before they are ready to leave residential care.

The majority of disabled young people who use short-term local authority residential care are accommodated for that period of time. Some, however, may be subject to care orders and live in foster care when they are not in short-term community homes.

Young people who are accommodated or in care (see below) for a consecutive period of three months, after their sixteenth birthday are entitled to advice, assistance and befriending up to the age of 21 years (Section 24, Children Act 1989).

In care

A care order (Section 31, Children Act 1989) is an order granted by a court which gives a local authority parental powers in relation to an individual young person up to her/his eighteenth birthday. The local authority, with this order, can continue to look after a young person against her or his parents' wishes. The order does not remove the parental responsibility of the young person's parents but it does give many powers to the local authority. There is, however, an expectation that the local authority will work in partnership with parents and young people.

Young people who have left care are entitled to the same advice, assistance and befriending services as young people who have been accommodated.

Detained

Young people can also be looked after by a local authority because:

- they have been remanded by a court following criminal charges;
- they have been arrested and detained by the police;

- they are subject to an emergency protection order, child assessment order or a criminal supervision order with residence requirements.

Young people who are detained by local authorities are eligible for advice, assistance and befriending when they are no longer looked after if they meet the criteria outlined above.

Reasons for young people entering care or accommodation

People think that if you're in care you must have done something wrong. The first question they ask is 'What did you do?' It's not just teachers and other kids at school but it's kids and staff in children's homes. When you go to a new place before you've got your foot in the door they say 'Hey, what are you in for?'

And yet the one thing I can't stand is people feeling sorry for us. That's worse than them thinking we're just a lot of yobbos.

(Page, R. and Clark, G.A. ed 1977, pp.16–17)

Two popular and contradictory images of young people who are looked after prevail in British society: one is the sad and lonely victim of abuse or disability; the other, more common representation is the wilful offender. The media is largely responsible for feeding these misconceptions and daily we are encouraged to vent anger and frustration at one set of young people (offenders) and pity and sympathy at another (victims). Both these constructions obscure the truth – young people who enter local authority residential care do so for a range of inter-related and complex reasons. These include:

- Family inability to care – resulting from illness, divorce, separation, death in family, or adults' inability to cope with their child's behaviour or disability for example. The inability of families to look after their children can be temporary or, less commonly, permanent;
- Abuse from parents or adults in their extended family (physical, sexual, emotional and/or psychological);
- Poverty and homelessness;
- No family contacts or support from community of origin (for example unaccompanied refugees or child immigrants);
- Concerns about aspects of young people's lifestyle or behaviour (for

example, young people who offend; travellers; young sex workers; persistent school refusers).

It will be unusual for a young person to be looked after for only one of the above reasons. For example, since the Children Act 1989 prevented local authorities from taking young people into care for non-school attendance, young people who refuse to attend school cannot be taken into care for this reason alone. The additional pressure which non-school attendance places on parents, or young people straying into offending, may be the factors which eventually lead to them being accommodated or in care. Similarly, young people from travelling families cannot be removed from their families because of their lifestyle. However, the difficulties which travelling families face in relation to public hostility, and recent changes in legislation in relation to local authority provision of sites, can prove overwhelming and lead to young people having to be looked after (Hodgkin, 1994).

Table 3: Factors affecting young people's entry to local authority care

Bebbington and Miles (1989) carried out a survey into the backgrounds of young people who entered care between 1 June and 30 November 1987.

Out of a sample of 2,528 young people they found that:

- only one-quarter of the young people were living with both parents before they came into care;

- almost three-quarters of their families were receiving income support;

- only one in five young people lived in owner-occupied housing;

- over half of the young people lived in deprived neighbourhoods.

This led the researchers to calculate the probabilities of young people entering care from two very different sets of circumstances:

Child A
Aged 5 to 9 ◆ Family not receiving income support ◆ Two parents living together ◆ Three or fewer children ◆ White ◆ Owner-occupied home ◆ More rooms in house than people.

Odds of entering care are 1 in 7,000

Child B
Aged 5 to 9 ◆ Family receiving income support ◆ One parent living with child ◆ Four or more children ◆ Mixed ethnic origin ◆ Private rented home ◆ One or more persons per room.

Odds of entering care are 1 in 10

For me [residential] care has been a positive experience. I believe that this was because of the relationships which I made and the support I was given. The time which I spent in care gave me the opportunity to develop as a person ... I knew that if I was unhappy about something I would have space to talk to someone individually with the knowledge they would take me seriously. In this way an environment was created which gave me a voice in the running of the home where I lived.

(Suraya Patel talking about her experiences of residential care in the 1980s in *Having a Voice, an Exploration of Children's Rights and Advocacy* 1995, pp.10–11)

I get on really well with the staff and the kids are really great. I enjoy the place I live and it's the first permanent place where I've been.

(15-year-old young woman in *Not Just a Name* 1993, p.84)

Residential care does not have to be the second or last option for young people, although it is often used this way. There will be some young people living in residential care who have never lived in foster care. A study carried out by the Dartington Social Research Unit (1984, p.80) reported that out of 450 young people admitted to care in five local authorities, 52 per cent were first placed in residential care. Rowe and others (1989) studied the placements of almost 6,000 young people in six authorities between 1985 and 1987. They found that 52 per cent of young people aged 11+ were placed in residential care, compared to six per cent of under four-year-olds (p.45). Many young people, particularly teenagers, do not want to live with foster carers because of their loyalty to their own families. Others will be concerned about the motivations of foster carers, or will prefer the freedom and space which group living can provide – both physically and emotionally. Some young people will pragmatically choose residential care over foster care because of experiences of placement breakdown in the latter: the study by Rowe and others cited above recorded the following placement disruptions (p.140).
(Continued on next page.)

Out of a sample of 3,763 placement endings:

percentage of foster placements which ended prematurely
    when child aged 5-10   20%
    when child aged 11+   38%

percentage of residential placements which ended prematurely
    when child aged 5-10   13%
    when child aged 11+   22%

Importantly, many young people who have lived in foster care report feeling like an 'outsider' or the 'odd one out'. A common complaint is that foster carers do not treat them the same as their natural children.

Chapter three
History and development of children's residential care

The provision of residential care for young people by local authorities has its historical roots in the 17th century. The 1601 Elizabethan Poor Law created workhouses for paupers. Here children were subject to the same harsh and punitive conditions as their adult contemporaries. Their days were long and hard and often filled with cruelty and abuse.

During the 19th century private and charitable boarding out schemes, orphanages, reformatory and charity schools were established. The Prevention of Cruelty to Children Act 1889 was the first piece of legislation preventing certain forms of cruelty to young people: similar protective legislation for animals had already existed for 60 years. Regulation of apprenticeships – where children frequently spent most of their waking hours cleaning chimneys and working in mines and factories – was also introduced. Many of today's leading children's charities – the National Society for the Prevention of Cruelty to Children, Barnardo's and NCH Action for Children, for example – were born during this period. These followed earlier initiatives to combat the social problems of the day; most notably the Thomas Coram Foundling Hospital, which was established in 1747 to provide shelter for unmarried mothers and illegitimate children.

The mission of the voluntary and religious societies of the 19th century was very clear: to rescue poor and destitute children from their appalling social conditions, lack of family care and unscrupulous adults who exploited them in various ways. However, the methods they employed would be largely scorned at today.

For example, the child-saving ideology of the Victorian era led to unquestioned belief in the efficacy of permanently separating children from their parents. An extreme consequence of this doctrine led to forced emigrations as far as Canada, Australia and South Africa. Between 1889 and 1909 voluntary societies officially posted 800 children to distant countries (Parker 1990, p.23) – almost a child a week for 20 years. Emigration of this kind continued until the 1960s. It is unlikely that any of these impoverished children had previously travelled outside their own towns or cities.

While reformers and individuals working during this generation may have been compassionate and caring, it is clear that the structural purpose of these 19th century institutions was to regulate, punish and reform individuals. For instance, the prevailing ideology of the 1834 Poor Law Amendment Act – whereby the notion of less eligibility ruled that no person receiving poor relief should be better off than the lowest paid worker – ensured that workhouses operated on subsistence rations, inhumane conditions and harsh physical labour. Improvements in pauper relief were officially disapproved as it was believed that better conditions would result in idleness and dependency.

The Poor Law system of pauper relief generally remained in place until the implementation of the Children Act 1948. It is therefore unsurprising that public perceptions of children's residential care are shaped by images of uniformed inmates scrubbing floors and asking for more (Parker 1990, p.1). During 1994 the author carried out a small study into the experiences of 65 young people in residential and foster care (Willow 1995). One of the questions related to young people's perceptions of residential care prior to entry. Many of their replies supported the view that public knowledge in this area is firmly rooted in the past:

'I thought that I'd have to sleep in a dormitory'

'I thought that I'd have to stay forever and would never see anyone again'

'I thought there would be whips, I'd have to scrub floors, clean windows and get no food'

'I had heard that in children's homes you are beat up and left in your rooms'

'[My mate told me] your head got stuffed down the loo and the chain flushed'

'My friends told me that you got locked in your room like a prison'

'I thought it would be like Oliver Twist or Annie!'

Thankfully the impressions of residential care which these young people had were soon proved inaccurate. These false images, nevertheless, added to the trauma and fear suffered by the young people who were not only distressed at what they were leaving behind but also by what they believed they were approaching. The recent Department of Health communication strategy to promote residential care should hopefully contribute to a better understanding among the general public.

The Children Act 1948 marked a watershed in the care of children separated from their families. The Act was significantly influenced by the Report of the Curtis Committee in 1946, which had been set up following a series of wartime scandals and the murder of a 13-year-old boy in 1945 by his foster father. Dennis O'Neill was beaten to death while living on his foster parents' farm in Shropshire. He had endured physical cruelty at the hands of his foster parent together with long periods of starvation; he weighed a mere four stones when he died. The Monckton Inquiry into this case added to the pressure for change.

Predictably the legislation which followed emphasised the need for training and the rights of young people to decent standards of care. Paradoxically, in the light of the O'Neill case, the 1948 Act promoted foster care over residential. Other influences – notably increased awareness of child development following World War II – stressed that children's need for attachment and individual care were more likely to be met in a family rather than group setting.

From 1951 to 1970 children's departments were responsible for the care of separated children: previously these responsibilities had been shared between different departments. A new post of Children's Officer was created with the express purpose of providing child-centred services and compensating children and young people for the loss of a normal home life.

The Seebohm Committee report of 1968 led to the creation of general social services departments in 1970. A significant piece of legislation followed in relation to young people's involvement – the Children Act 1975.

Section 59 of the Children Act 1975 for the first time stated that local authorities should consult with young people in care before making decisions affecting them:

in reaching any decision relating to a child in their care, a local authority shall give first consideration to the need to safeguard and promote the welfare of the child throughout his childhood: and shall so far as is practicable ascertain the wishes and feelings of the child regarding the decision and give due weight according to his age and understanding

The following quote from a Social Work Today article in 1979 illustrates some of the reactions to this Act:

Children in residential care are just becoming aware of the Children Act 1975 which gives them a right to consultation about decisions affecting their welfare. They are marching in the streets claiming their rights and some have resorted to direct action in barricading themselves in a home due to be closed

(Walton cited in Crompton 1980, p.41)

This requirement to consult and involve young people in making decisions was retained as Section 18(1) of the Child Care Act 1980 and as Sections 22(3) and (5) of the Children Act 1989.

Developments in children's residential care; an overview

Children's residential care has undergone a number of transformations over the last 50 years. The developments can be summarised under three headings: purpose of residential care; perceptions of young people who live in residential care; and people who work in residential care.

Purpose of residential care

Unlike the large institutions of the last century, the purpose of residential care in the 1990s is not to provide shelter only or to punish. The Children Act 1989 guidance on residential care from the Department of Health clearly requires that all young people who are looked after have their individual needs met and their rights respected, irrespective of the type of residential placement.

Knowledge about human development and young people's needs has significantly increased over the last five decades. Social work has been heavily influenced by research in the social sciences, particularly after World War II during which, for example, much was learnt about the effects of separation upon children and young people. During the last two decades in particular, research has increasingly been available.

In contemporary society, residential care is divorced from systems of income maintenance and poor relief. It is described within legislation as a means of supporting children and families. The official emphasis is upon treating young people as individuals rather than members of groups: the perils of institutionalism are known and their avoidance encouraged.

Young people who live in residential homes

Unlike 50 years ago, the majority of young people who live in local authority residential care leave after relatively short periods of time. Their parents and other relatives will continue to be the most significant people in their lives and most will maintain frequent contact with them. The majority of new entrants to residential care are young people in their teenage years. They will enter only after other social work community resources have failed. Young people who live in residential care form the minority of the 'looked after' population; the majority of their contemporaries are in foster care.

Insufficient data on the numbers of disabled young people living in local authority residential care means that it is impossible to say whether the shift in social services toward family-based care has included them. The majority of the 45,000 disabled young people which Russell (1994) estimated to be living in residential care are in educational institutions. Residential care has remained the main type of care for disabled young people living away from their families while their non-disabled contemporaries can, on the whole, expect to be placed in families. More research is obviously needed in this area (Morris 1995, pp.90-93).

Young people who live in residential homes are not exclusively from poor families, although the chances of living in any form of state care are greatly affected by poverty (see Table 3, p.12). Massive efforts since 1948 have been made to reduce the stigma and isolation of care and the lives of young people in residential care are expected to bear close resemblance to their peers. Emphasis in the social sciences has shifted from the deficiencies of individual young people and their families to the deficiencies of society. More recently the concept of rights for young people, including in residential care, has evolved.

People who work in residential care

Since the creation of the Children's Departments in 1950, there has been a steady professionalisation of social work with children and young people, particularly in the fieldwork sector. While residential workers have never been required to hold a professional social work qualification, there has always been a general consensus that this is desirable. Training for residential child care staff was introduced by the Home Office in 1947 ahead of training for field social workers. The Warner report (1992) has had a significant influence in promoting good practice in the selection, training and supervision of residential staff. At the very least, people choosing to work in residential care are now expected to have a good understanding of human growth and development and the needs and rights of young people (Support Force 1995a).

As a society we have had to accept that adults' motivations for working with young people in many contexts are not always good ones. A glance at national newspapers or social work journals – where we can regularly read of assaults on young people in various forms of care – is a poignant reminder of the vigilance required when recruiting, selecting and managing residential staff and foster carers.

The tremendous range of skills and commitment required of residential workers has been recognised in major reports (Levy and Kahan 1991; Utting 1991; Howe 1992; Skinner 1992; Warner 1992) and the need for specialist training has also been acknowledged.

From workhouse to Warner: what has changed for young people?

While the conditions of young people living in local authority residential care are unquestionably better than their predecessors in 1948, there is still a great deal to be done to improve young people's experiences of residential care. Despite the recent proliferation of interest in children's residential care, and the wealth of reports, inquiries and guidance, young people in the 1990s continue to raise similar concerns to their predecessors 20 years ago. The themes commonly raised by young people over the last two decades include their rights to:

- be heard
- be treated as individuals
- be given respect and privacy
- be treated with fairness and consistency
- make choices
- be seen and treated as 'normal'.

Exercise: Changes in residential care

The following can be completed by individual members of staff as preparation for a team discussion on developments in children's residential care. The form may then be photocopied for distribution.

Time-span you have worked in residential care   19   to   19

What changes have you observed in your work in children's residential care?

_____

_____

_____

_____

_____

What changes have you observed in young people who live in residential care?

_____

_____

_____

_____

_____

What changes have you observed in staff in children's residential care?

_____

_____

_____

_____

_____

Discussion points

- What have been the positive aspects of recent developments in residential care?

- What have been the negative aspects of recent developments in residential care?

- What impact have these changes had on your practice?

- If you were in charge, what further developments or changes would you institute in:
  i)   your residential home?
  ii)   all homes in your local authority?
  iii)   residential care nationally?

Chapter four
Children's rights in residential care

Defining rights

It is not uncommon nowadays to hear young people declare that they have rights: often this is set within the context of a dispute or disagreement with a person in authority – a parent, a teacher or a social worker, for example. However this rarely reflects an in-depth knowledge of their various legal entitlements. Here young people – like other groups before them – are employing the language of rights as a shorthand way of asserting their value and worth *as human beings*.

When we talk about promoting children's rights we are usually making two separate points. The first is that we believe that young people everywhere have rights as human beings and should be treated with equal respect to adults. Secondly we are referring to the legal rights or entitlements which young people actually have in law.

Legal rights or entitlements are not static – they change all the time. Even today where young people in residential care have many legal rights there are individuals and groups of people – young and old – who are canvassing for yet more improvements.

When considering the legal rights of young people who live in residential care it is necessary to refer to the Children Act 1989 and the associated guidance and regulations. Young people who are looked after have additional legal entitlements relating to education, health, housing, social security and civil and political rights.

Rights in residential care: where did they come from?

There is no doubt that developments in residential care over the last 50 years have been far-reaching. Not only have massive structural changes occurred in relation to the numbers, types and purposes of homes but there has also been a clear ideological movement towards viewing young people in general, and those who live in residential care specifically, as people with rights.

Who Cares?

The rights or entitlements of young people who live in residential care have evolved partly because of collective action by young people (Collins, S. and Stein, M. in Rojek and others 1989, pp. 84-108). In June 1975 the National Children's Bureau organised a one-day *Who Cares?* conference, attended by 100 young people between the ages of 12 and 16. Following this successful initiative, a group of 16 young people – the *Who Cares? Young People's Working Group* – continued to meet for another year and produced the first national publication of young people's views in care (Page, R. and Clark, G.A. 1977).

This charter was written by the Who Cares? Young People's Working Group in the 1970s. How relevant is it today?

Charter of rights for young people in care

We have drawn up this charter for 'young people' because we feel it is the responsibility of the residential worker and social worker to make sure that younger kids get a good deal.

1. The right to be accepted and treated as an individual member of society. Also the right to be treated with the same respect given to any other valid member of the human race.

2. The right to know who we are. To know our parents and brothers and sisters. To have factual information about our family origins and background.

3. The right to be able to make our own decisions and to have real influence over those decisions we are sometimes considered too thick to participate in.

4. The right to privacy. We understand that in care it is not always possible to choose who we are going to live and share our lives with. But we are still human beings and are still entitled to the essential amount of privacy needed before cracking up.

5. The right to be given an insight into the use of money by handling it, using it and paying the consequences if we misuse it, eg, being given the money in our hand to buy the clothes our clothing allowance will allow.

6. The right to choose those who will represent us whether it be legally or otherwise, eg, social workers. Also the right to choose those whom we wish to confide in.

7. Finally, the right to be as much a part of society as the next person and not to be labelled in any way. In short, to live.

These rights can be interpreted how you like. But don't misuse them or distort them for your own devices.

(taken from Page, R. and Clark, G.A.1977, p.62)

Who Cares? Magazine for young people in the care system

In 1978 a Who Cares? group was set up in the London borough of Westminster. Tory Laughland, who was to become the founder and first director of the Who Cares? Trust 14 years later, was then a social worker and part of the group. In 1983 the group decided to produce a local magazine about being in care and Tory was its editor. Four years later Who Cares? moved to the National Children's Bureau and became a national magazine – with readers in Japan, the USA and Finland. By 1994 the magazine had a distribution of 30,000 – over half the population of all young people looked after in England and Wales (information obtained from Who Cares? magazine issue 29, Autumn 1994).

National Association of Young People in Care

When the funding for the National Children's Bureau Who Cares? project ended in 1979, the National Association of Young People in Care (NAYPIC) was formed. NAYPIC campaigned for various improvements in care between June 1979 and 1994 when it ceased to function. The aims of NAYPIC were to:

- promote the views and opinions of young people in care and those who had left care;
- offer advice and assistance to young people in care and ex-care;
- educate the public and child care professionals on matters relating to young people in care and those who had left care.

Membership of NAYPIC was open only to people who were, or who had been, in care under the age of 25 years, although adults were involved in an advisory capacity. Three of the organisation's major campaigns related to:

i)   the negative effect on young people of bulk-buying in residential care (toiletries, clothes and food) and the use of vouchers;

ii)   the need for open access to social services files;

iii) young people's right to attend their reviews.

Funded by the Department of Health, NAYPIC was a national organisation with regional offices at various times in Bradford, Coventry, Liverpool, London, Manchester and Southampton.

NAYPIC gave significant written and verbal evidence about all aspects of care in 1983/84 to the House of Commons Select Committee on Social Services in its work on children in care. The Committee's report led eventually to the Children Act 1989.

Black and in care

Another important organisation during the 1980s was Black and In Care. In October 1984 a national conference was held in London for black young people, social workers and community workers. The conference was jointly organised by black people who were, or had been, in care, NAYPIC and the Children's Legal Centre. Workshops for young people looked at:

- culture, hair and skin
- mixed parentage
- racism in the care system
- fostering
- leaving care.

A conference report was produced which, together with a video *Black and In Care*, has had a significant impact in raising awareness among social workers.

Black and In Care

This poignant poem was written by Margaret Parr 11 years ago – how have things changed since then?

It's bad for your child to be in care

I can't face this life alone

'cos I've always lived in a home

Thrown out at seventeen

with no friends or family

Thank-you social services

for your hospitality.

Here I am in a black community

I've grown up 'white' but they can't see.

Which do I turn to – white or black?

I daren't step forward, I can't step back

Help me someone please

To find my culture and identity

Why could I not have these when I was young?

They brought me up to think being black is wrong.

Black people out there

You've got to be aware

For it's bad for your child to be in care.

(taken from *Black and In Care* conference report 1985)

Research into young people's views

During 1970 Barbara Kahan, then Oxfordshire's Children's Officer, and two training officers spent 11 Saturday mornings with ten adults aged between 19 and 34 years talking about their care experiences. The discussions were tape-recorded and used as the basis for a book *Growing Up in Care: Ten people talking* (Kahan, 1979). In her final paragraph, Kahan persuasively encourages readers to value and listen to those who have been in care:

> *Amongst the community there must be a very large number of ex-children in care who are now living their lives, rearing their children and carrying forward with them, as we all do, the experiences they had when they were children. They may have important news to offer, good and bad, with lessons that should be learned by policy-makers, professional service providers, training agencies and the public as a whole. There is evidence that they might be willing to tell us the news. Should we not give them the opportunity?*

More recently, Jenny Morris (1995) has carried out research into the childhood experiences of disabled adults. By advertising in newsletters of local disability groups, and using informal networks, Morris was able to record the experiences 10 people had of residential and foster care from the 1950s onwards. She explains (p.5):

> *the purpose of including these stories is to give a voice to experiences which we don't know enough about.*

Further reading

Since the 1970s a number of studies, books and reports of young people's experiences in residential and foster care have been published. The majority of these included the views of young people currently living in residential care while some involved adults looking back on their lives in care.

Page, R and Clark, GA (1977) *Who Cares? Young People in Care Speak Out.* National Children's Bureau

Kahan, B (1979) *Growing Up in Care, Ten People Talking.* Basil Blackwell

Stein, M and Ellis, S (1983) *'Gizza Say', Reviews and Young People in Care.* National Association of Young People in Care

Denton, G (1985) *For Whose Eyes Only, Files and Young People in* Care. National Association of Young People in Care

Stein, M and Maynard, C (1985) *I've Never Been So Lonely.* National Association of Young People in Care

Black and In Care Steering Group (1985) *Black and In Care Conference Report.* Children's Legal Centre

Fisher, M, Marsh, P and Phillips, D (1986) *In and Out of Care, the Experience of Children, Parents and Social Workers.* Batsford/BAAF

Gardner, R (1987) *Who Says? Choice and Control in Care.* National Children's Bureau

Nottinghamshire County Council (1992) *As if They Were Our Own. Raising the Quality of Residential Child Care in Nottinghamshire: the Report of the Chief Executive's Working Party*

Hampshire County Council (1993) *Listening to Children.* Hampshire County Council Social Services Department

Wheal, A and Buchanan, (1993) *Answering Back, Report by Young people being Looked After on the Children Act 1989.* University of Southampton

Fletcher, B (1993) *Not Just a Name, the Views of Young People in Foster and Residential Care.* National Consumer Council

Butler, I and Williamson, H (1994) *Children Speak, Children, Trauma and Social Work.* Longmans

Morris, S and Wheatley, H (1994) *Time to Listen, the Experiences of Children in Residential and Foster Care.* Childline

Lynes, D and Goddard, J (1995) *The View from the Front, the User-View of Childcare in Norfolk.* Norfolk County Council Social Services Department

Morris, J (1995) *Gone Missing? A Research and Policy Review of Disabled Children Living Away from their Families.* Who Cares? Trust

Safe and Sound (1995) *So Who are we Meant to Trust Now? Responding to Abuse in Care: the Experiences of Young people.* NSPCC

Riddell, M (1996) *The Cornflake Kid.* Partnership Publications

Exercise: Listening to, and learning from, the experiences of young people

As a staff team, select two of the above publications and identify individuals within your group to read them and prepare a summary of the main points:

- how were the young people's views collected – for example: by holding a meeting or conference; by individual interviews or questionnaires?
- how many young people were consulted, or involved?
- when were the young people in care or accommodated, in what type of care, and for how long?
- what were the positive experiences of these young people?
- what were the negative experiences of these young people?
- are there any particular quotes or messages that stand out?

A team discussion could then address the following two questions:

(i)   if the young people who currently live in your home were asked to participate in a similar study or project, what would they say about their care?

(ii) how can you develop your practice to incorporate the wealth of information that exists about young people's experiences of care and accommodation?

The above exercise can be repeated on a six-monthly cycle

Children's rights in the 1990s

In-care groups

The first local in-care group was the Leeds AdLib group which ran from 1973 to 1975 (Collins, S. and Stein, M. 1989, p.100). Two decades later, there are over 30 in-care groups in England and Wales (Patel, S. 1995). These local groups, while offering support, friendship and advice to their members, frequently attempt to influence the policies and practices of local authorities in relation to residential and foster care.

Children's rights officers

A welcome development for children's rights in care came in 1987 when Leicestershire County Council appointed Mike Lindsay, who had formerly been in care himself, as the United Kingdom's first children's rights officer. There are now 28 children's rights and advocacy officers in England and Wales (Children's Rights Officers and Advocates 1995). The purpose of children's rights services are, generally, to provide independent advocacy, support and representation to young people who are looked after in various settings. Most children's rights and advocacy officers have regular and frequent contact with young people and offer advice and information to help resolve difficulties.

While some local authorities, for example, Berkshire, Birmingham and Leicestershire have located children's rights services within their social services departments, the majority, including Hackney, Leeds and Rochdale, have entered into partnerships with voluntary child care organisations to establish some independence for them. This development has certain advantages in relation to their autonomy from local authorities but there are notable disadvantages associated with accessibility to local authority information and records (Ellis, S. and Franklin, A. 1995, p.91).

Formed in 1992, Children's Rights Officers and Advocates (CROA) exists to:

- develop and promote a set of principles for all children's rights officers and advocates;
- develop and promote high standards of professional practice amongst children's rights officers and advocates;

- encourage other local authorities, and voluntary child care agencies, to establish children's rights and advocacy services;
- provide advice, information and support services to its members;
- seek to influence the policies of local and national government and statutory and other agencies in respect of children's rights;
- develop and promote a wider interest in, understanding of, and respect for children's rights work and the professional role of children's rights and advocacy officers.

Local support services

There are other specialist posts which have been created within local authorities to safeguard and promote young people's rights in care and accommodation (see Table Four, pp. 35–36). These include the Young Person's Forum Co-ordinator in Birmingham, a unique post which is only open to people who have lived in local authority care or accommodation. Louise Bessant, the first and current postholder, has a key role in advocating on behalf of young people who are looked after both regionally and nationally.

Independent representatives are available to young people who are in secure accommodation while independent visitors are available to young people who are looked after if they have had no contact with their families for over a year. Independent persons are laypeople who assist with the investigation of complaints. Some local authorities, for example Leicestershire, have established specialist posts for the investigation of complaints and allegations of abuse in residential and foster care.

National support services

In addition to support services locally, young people in residential care have access to Childline and Who Cares? telephone lines as well as national organisations such as Advice, Advocacy and Representation Services for Children (ASC) and Voice for the Child in Care (VCC). In Wales and Scotland, Voices from Care and Who Cares? Scotland are organisations established and run mainly by young people who are, or who have been, in local authority care or accommodation. A list of these organisations is given on pp.113–115.

As well as providing critical support services for young people who are looked after, national organisations can play an important role in informing social work policy and practice. For example, in 1994 Childline produced a report, *Time to Listen*, describing the types of issues raised by the 676 young people in care who used their freephone between October 1992 and March 1993. Valerie Howarth, the organisation's director, summarised their findings:

> *A constant theme in their conversation has been their sense of abandonment, unimportance and low self-esteem* Morris, S. and Wheatley, H. (1994, p.12)

Glenthorne youth treatment centre

In 1991 the Secretary of State for Health set up a special group to ensure that young people living in the Department of Health youth treatment centres were being looked after properly. The remit of this group was to 'watch over their (St. Charles and Glenthorne centres) care practices with particular regard to children's rights'. This followed grave concerns about the running of the St. Charles centre in Essex, the closure of which the Department of Health has since announced.

All the above combine to provide a range of essential support services for young people who are looked after. While some services are provided to help specifically with resolving problems and difficulties, others offer a listening ear and friendship. This is a great improvement on the paucity of independent services available to young people in care in previous decades.

The appalling treatment and systematic abuse of young people in Staffordshire and Leicestershire (Levy, A. and Kahan, B. 1991; Kirkwood, A. 1993) residential homes were exposed in the early 1990s while further coverage of other abuses has sensitised the public and social care professionals to the fact that without proper resources, safeguards, supervision and management, the public, voluntary and private care of young people can be extremely damaging. Any effort to prevent the terrible events which occurred in Staffordshire, Leicestershire and other settings happening again needs to ensure that:

- staff selected to work in (and with) residential homes are properly vetted, trained and supported;
- all residential homes develop cultures where young people's rights are known, respected and promoted;
- trusted adults outside of the care system are available to all young people who are looked after.

Table 4 shows the range of independent services for young people who live in residential care. The term independent can mean different things. For instance, it can refer to services where staff are:

- **located in an arms-length unit within a social services department**
  for example, children's rights officers, investigating officers for complaints and guardians ad litem;
- **managed by a voluntary child care organisation on behalf of a local authority**
  for example, children's rights and advocacy officers, independent visitors, representatives and persons;
- **expected to operate independently from the rest of the organisation although they are still employed by and located within it**
  for example, people who are employed to independently chair and monitor reviews;
- **responsible for carrying out a specific task independently**
  for example, staff who chair reviews in addition to other responsibilities.

Table 4: Independent services for young people who live in residential care

Type of service:	Available to:	Service	Provided by:
children's rights and advocacy officers	young people who are looked after some children's rights and advocacy officers also provide a service to 'children in need'	independent advice, advocacy and representation	28 local authorities in England and Wales (the majority of children's rights and advocacy services are managed by voluntary child care organisations)
investigating officer for complaints	young people who make formal complaints under Children Act 1989	impartial investigation of complaint (with independent person)	all local authorities in England and Wales
guardians ad litem	appointed by courts for young people who are the subject of specified proceedings under Children Act 1989	represent young people's interests (not necessarily wishes) in court proceedings	all local authorities in England and Wales
independent person	young people who make formal complaints under Children Act 1989	independent investigation of complaint (with investigating officer)	all local authorities in England and Wales (Voice for the Child in Care also provide this service in partnership with local authorities)

independent representatives	young people who live in secure accommodation and Glenthorne youth treatment centre	independent advice, representation, support and advocacy	Voice for the Child in Care (contracted by local authorities)
independent reviewing officers	all young people who are looked after	chair statutory reviews and ensure that care plan decisions are implemented	all local authorities in England and Wales some local authorities – for example, Birmingham – have established specialist independent reviewing units whose staff have no other responsibilities within the organisation
independent visitors	young people who are looked after and either have had no contact with their parents for over 12 months, or have infrequent communication with them	independent advice and befriending	all local authorities in England and Wales (some independent visitor schemes are managed by voluntary child care organisations)

While the list above highlights independent services available to young people, it is important to remember the support and help which young people can receive from their parents, families, friends and local in-care groups.

The next three chapters illustrate the rights which young people who live in residential care have according to the:

- United Nations Convention on the Rights of the Child;
- Children Act 1989 (primary legislation);
- guidance and regulations (secondary legislation).

This information has been included so that readers can gain a full understanding of young people's entitlements and also appreciate the common features and overlap between the UN Convention and the Children Act 1989.

Both the UN Convention and the Children Act 1989 came into force in the United Kingdom in 1991. A summary of these important pieces of legislation is provided together with some direct extracts and ideas about their implementation in a residential setting.

Chapter five
The United Nations Convention on the Rights of the Child

The United Nations Convention on the Rights of the Child was ratified, with four reservations, by the United Kingdom on 12 December 1991. The Convention, which has the status of international law, affects all people under the age of 18 years.

The Convention has been produced for all 191 countries of the world. There are great differences in wealth and poverty between countries in the northern and southern hemispheres. For affluent countries like the United Kingdom, many of the welfare provisions of the Convention are already embodied by national legislation. When considering how the Articles of the Convention apply to young people who live in residential care, there is therefore much overlap between the Convention and the Children Act 1989. The Convention in this respect supports and adds weight to domestic law.

Over 180 countries have gone through the process of ratification – which means that they have agreed to be bound by the Convention.

In 1994 the UK Government presented its first report to the UN Committee on the Rights of the Child and was subject to much criticism because of, for example, recent developments in juvenile justice and proposals concerning secure training centres.

There are 54 Articles in the Convention – 40 ascribe direct rights to young people. These rights can be categorised under three broad headings – rights to welfare provision, protection and participation. What follows is a list of 24 Articles which most directly affect young people who live in residential care.

Article 1   Definition of a child
Article 2   Right to non-discrimination
Article 3   Right to have best interests taken into account
Article 8   Right to identity
Article 9   Rights when separated from parents
Article 10   Right to family reunification
Article 12   Right to express views and opinions
Article 13   Right to freedom of expression
Article 14   Right to freedom of thought, conscience and religion
Article 19   Right to protection from abuse and neglect
Article 20   Right to protection for young people without families
Article 22   Rights of young people who are refugees
Article 23   Rights of young people who are disabled
Article 24   Right to health information and services
Article 25   Right to periodic review of placement
Article 26   Right to social security
Article 27   Right to adequate standard of living
Article 28   Right to education
Article 29   Aims of education
Article 30   Rights of young people from minority ethnic communities
Article 31   Rights to leisure, recreation and cultural activities
Article 37   Torture and deprivation of liberty
Article 39   Rights to rehabilitative care
Article 40   Rights of young people who have allegedly committed
             offences

Full copies of the Convention can be obtained from the Children's Legal Centre or the Children's Rights Office (see pp. 115–116).

	Summary of relevant Articles of the UN Convention on the Rights of the Child	Implementing the UN Convention in residential care
Definition of a child	**Article 1** The UN Convention applies to all people from birth to the age of 18 years	
Right to non-discrimination	**Article 2** Staff need to take action to ensure that young people who live in residential care are not discriminated against	**Example:** staff can ensure that young people are not discriminated against by liaising and forming positive relationships with local schools and neighbours; making opportunities available to young people which their peers not living in residential care expect and enjoy
Right to have best interests as a primary consideration	**Article 3** All actions affecting young people must have their best interests as the primary consideration In a residential setting young people's needs must have equal priority with the needs of the staff, or of the home itself	**Example:** staff rotas should be designed to ensure continuity of care for young people – for example, by making sure that the staff who were on duty when young people went to bed are there the next morning to wake them up
Right to identity	**Article 8** Young people are entitled to preserve their identity Staff need to promote the identities of young people who live in residential homes	**Example:** staff can help young people preserve their identity by helping them to prepare life-story books, collect photographs, retrieve important documents, including birth certificates and maintain contact with family and friends

Rights when separated from parents	**Article 9** Contact between young people and their parents needs to be encouraged and facilitated If contact between a young person and her/his parents is terminated this must be in the best interests of the young person	**Example:** staff can encourage contact by ensuring that there is a comfortable room in the home where young people and their families can meet in private; helping young people write letters and providing stationery and stamps; ensuring that there is a space in the home where young people can make and receive private telephone calls
Right to family reunification	**Article 10** Young people have the right to leave or enter a country for the purpose of family reunification Young people whose parents live in different countries have the right to maintain regular contact with both parents	**Example:** residential staff can promote direct (visits and holidays) and indirect (letters; telephone calls; cards and exchange of photographs) contact between young people and their parents, siblings and extended family
Right to express views and opinions	**Article 12** All young people should be allowed to express their views and opinions	**Example:** in a residential setting, young people can be encouraged to participate in residents' meetings, reviews, planning meetings and case conferences, local authority inspections and visits by elected members
Right to freedom of expression	**Article 13** Young people should have the freedom to express themselves so long as they do not infringe the rights of others	**Example:** in residential care, young people's privacy should be respected when making and receiving telephone calls, sending and receiving letters, displaying material (posters, artwork, photographs) in their bedrooms and communal areas

Right to freedom of thought, conscience and religion	**Article 14** The religious and other beliefs of young people should be respected Parental influence on young people's beliefs should be respected	**Example:** staff can show respect for young people's religious and other beliefs by ensuring that appropriate food is provided, making space available in the home for religious worship and providing transport (or paying fares) to and from places of worship Staff can demonstrate respect for young people's parents by encouraging and enabling contact, enquiring after them and learning about their views and lifestyles
Right to protection from abuse and neglect	**Article 19** Staff have a responsibility to ensure that young people who live in residential care are protected from abuse and neglect	**Example:** staff can initiate discussions with individual and groups of young people about bullying and racist and sexist behaviour; organisations can ensure that young people have access to independent people who will support and advise them
Rights of young people without families to protection	**Article 20** When young people cannot live in a family environment, they are entitled to 'special protection and assistance' Particular attention needs to be directed at ensuring continuity in young people's lives and to their ethnic, religious, cultural and linguistic background	**Example:** keyworker systems in residential care can provide individual young people with a member of staff who will take special responsibility for, and interest in, her/his care and development

Rights of young people who are refugees	**Article 22** When young people who are refugees are placed in residential care this Article of the Convention will apply Young people who are refugees are entitled to protection and humanitarian assistance. This includes help to trace and return to their parents and families, where appropriate	**Example:** residential staff can make special efforts to ensure that refugee young people are reunified with their parents or families through discussions in planning meetings and reviews
Rights of disabled young people	**Article 23** Disabled young people are entitled to dignity, independence and participation; active participation in the community; and the fullest possible social integration and individual development	**Example:** residential staff can promote this Article by ensuring that young people have privacy when bathing and dressing or undressing; encouraging young people to make everyday decisions and choices, as well as long- term plans for their future; seeking to involve young people in the running of the home and in local leisure and community activities; ensuring that young people have maximum social integration with their peers and mainstream services
Right to health and health services	**Article 24** Young people have the right to good standards of health and to services which promote their health	**Example:** staff can promote young people's health in residential care by providing and raising awareness about nutritious food; encouraging exercise and fitness; ensuring that all young people are registered with a general practitioner and dentist; encouraging, where necessary, young people to have their sight tested and wear spectacles or contact lenses; ensuring that young people attend hospital outpatient appointments and take medication, where appropriate

Right to periodic review of placement	**Article 25** Young people are entitled to have their care periodically reviewed	**Example:** staff can encourage young people to attend and participate in their statutory reviews by ensuring that they are consulted about the time and venue of meetings; helping young people prepare in advance what they want to say; reading through social work and school reports with young people before the meeting and asking whether they would like a friend or advocate to attend (Wheal and Sinclair's recent publication *It's YOUR Meeting* (1995) is an invaluable tool for helping young people prepare for their reviews)
Right to social security	**Article 26** Young people are entitled to social security benefits	**Example:** in order to apply for social security benefits young people must have national insurance numbers. These are automatically sent to young people whose parents are in receipt of child benefit. Residential staff will therefore need to help young people living in residential care to get their national insurance numbers before they make claims for social security benefits
Right to adequate standard of living	**Article 27** Young people have a right to an adequate standard of living Staff need to take steps to ensure that young people who live in residential care have their physical, mental, spiritual, moral and social needs met	**Example:** individual care plans for young people should address the standards of care in the home, and whether the diverse needs of individual young people are being met

Right to education	**Article 28** All young people are entitled to education Steps need to be taken to ensure that young people regularly attend school	**Example:** staff in residential homes can take an active interest in young people's education by forging positive links with local schools; ensuring that each young person has a private place to study and appropriate materials (pens and pencils, stationery, desk or table, reading lamp); encouraging membership of local libraries; talking with young people and asking about school; being positive role-models and valuing education as a lifelong process rather than simply associating it with school attendance
Aims of education	**Article 29** The aims of education are to promote the full development of individuals in a social climate of understanding, tolerance and friendship	**Example:** staff can encourage young people to feel good about themselves and recognise their talents by constantly praising their achievements at home, school and work; encouraging special interests and hobbies and ensuring that young people know they have rights
Rights of young people from minority ethnic communities	**Article 30** Young people from minority ethnic communities are entitled to enjoy their own culture, religion and language	**Example:** staff can promote the rights of young people from minority ethnic communities by encouraging contact between young people and their families and local communities; ensuring that pictures, books, newspapers, magazines and videos and music are representative of different cultures; helping young people to attend places of worship and encouraging them to use their first language, using interpreters where necessary
Rights to leisure, recreation and cultural activities	**Article 31** All young people have the right to play, leisure and recreation	**Example:** staff can promote young people's rights to leisure, recreation and cultural activities by visits to museums, libraries, play parks and leisure centres, theatres and cinemas

Torture and deprivation of liberty	**Article 37** Young people can never be subjected to torture or other cruel treatment or punishment Depriving young people of their liberty should be a measure of last resort, and for as short a period of time as possible Young people deprived of their liberty are entitled to maintain contact with their families and to legal representation	**Example:** staff can promote this Article by ensuring that young people have access to good solicitors. Staff can encourage contact with families by using methods outlined in Articles 9 and 10
Right to rehabilitative care	**Article 39** Young people who have been neglected, exploited or subject to some other form of abuse or punishment, should be helped to recover in an atmosphere which promotes their self-respect and dignity	**Example:** staff can promote this right by respecting young people and encouraging and praising their achievements. Consulting and involving young people in everyday decision making is an ideal means of raising their self confidence and esteem

Rights of young people who have allegedly committed offences	**Article 40**	**Example:** staff in residential homes can promote this right by ensuring that young people know their legal entitlements and have access to good solicitors and interpreters and by ensuring that young people know about and can access the range of support services available to them
	Young people who have, or allegedly have, committed criminal offences are to be treated with respect and dignity so that they can be reintegrated into society	
	All young people who are accused of committing offences are innocent until proven guilty	
	All young people are entitled to legal representation	
	Interpreters should be available to young people who do not understand or speak the national language	
	States should set a standard age below which no person can be charged with infringing the criminal law	
	States should respond to young people who offend by a package of measures which are divorced from the courts and criminal proceedings	

Chapter six
The Children Act 1989

What follows is an outline of the main features of the Children Act 1989 in relation to young people's entitlements. The right column provides direct extracts from the Act; the left column summarises the provisions.

Young people with sufficient understanding can apply to courts for orders relating to who they live with (residence order) and who they have contact with (contact order).

Section 10 (8)

Where the person applying for leave to make an application for a section 8 order is the child concerned, the court may only grant leave if it is satisfied that he has sufficient understanding to make the proposed application for the section 8 order.

Social workers should consult young people prior to making decisions about them.

Local authorities must take into account young people's religious persuasion, racial and cultural and linguistic background.

Section 22 (4)

Before making any decision with respect to a child whom they are looking after, or proposing to look after, a local authority shall, so far as is reasonably practicable, ascertain the wishes of-
(a)   the child;
(b)   his parents;
(c)   any person who is not a parent of his but who has parental responsibility for him; and
(d)   any other person whose wishes and feelings the authority consider to be relevant, regarding the matter to be decided.

Section 22 (5)

In making any such decision a local authority shall give due consideration-
(a)   having regard to his age and understanding, to such wishes and feelings of the child as they have been able to ascertain;
(b)   to such wishes and feelings of any person

mentioned in subsection (4)(b) to (d) as they have been able to ascertain; and
(c) to the child's religious persuasion, racial origin and cultural and linguistic background.

Young people who are looked after should be accommodated near their home and with their siblings if it is in their best interests.

Section 23 (7)

Where a local authority provides accommodation for a child whom they are looking after, they shall, subject to the provisions of this Part and so far as is reasonably practicable and consistent with his welfare, secure that
(a) the accommodation is near his home; and
(b) where the authority are also providing accommodation for a sibling of his, they are accommodated together.

Homes for disabled young people should be adapted to meet their needs, as far as is reasonably practicable.

Section 23 (8)

Where a local authority provide accommodation for a child whom they are looking after and who is disabled, they shall, so far as is reasonably practicable, ensure that the accommodation is not unsuitable to his particular needs.

Young people who are looked after have a right to advice, assistance and befriending up to the age of 21.

Section 24 (1)

Where a child is being looked after by a local authority, it shall be the duty of the authority to advise, assist and befriend him with a view to promoting his welfare when he ceases to be looked after by them.

Section 24 (2)

In this Part 'a person qualifying for advice and assistance' means a person within the area of the authority who is under twenty-one and who was, at any time after reaching the age of sixteen but while still a child-
(a) looked after by a local authority;
(b) accommodated by or on behalf of a voluntary organisation;
(c) accommodated in a registered children's home;
(d) accommodated-

(i) by any health authority or local education authority

(ii) in any residential care home, nursing home or mental nursing home [or in any accommodation provided by a National Health Service Trust],

for a consecutive period of at least three months; or

(e) privately fostered,

but who is no longer so looked after, accommodated or fostered.

Section 24 (8)

A local authority may give assistance to any person who qualifies for advice and assistance by virtue of subsection (2)(a) by-

(a) contributing to expenses incurred by him in living near the place where he is, or will be –

(i) employed or seeking employment; or

(ii) receiving education or training; or

(b) making a grant to enable him to meet expenses connected with his education or training.

Section 24 (9)

Where a local authority are assisting the person under subsection (8) by making a contribution or grant with respect to a course of education or training, they may-

(a) continue to do so even though he reaches the age of 21 before completing the course; and

(b) disregard any interruption in his attendance on the course if he resumes it as soon as is reasonably practicable.

Young people can only be placed in secure accommodation if they meet certain criteria.

Section 25 (1)

Subject to the following provisions of this section, a child who is being looked after by a local authority may not be placed, and, if placed may not be kept, in accommodation provided for the purpose of restricting liberty ('secure accommodation') unless it appears-

(a) that-

(i) he has a history of absconding and is

likely to abscond from any other
description of accommodation; and

    (ii) if he absconds, he is likely to suffer
significant harm; or

(b)   that if he is kept in any other description of
accommodation he is likely to injure
himself, or other persons.

Young people have a right to
make a complaint if they are not
happy with the services they
receive.

Section 26 (3)

Every local authority shall establish a procedure
for considering any representations (including
any complaint) made to them by-

(a)   any child who is being looked after by them
or who is not being looked after by them
but is in need;

(b)   a parent of his;

(c)   any person who is not a parent of his but
who has parental responsibility for him;

(d)   any local authority foster parent;

(e)   such other person as the authority consider
has a sufficient interest in the child's
welfare to warrant his representations
being considered by them,

about the discharge by the authority of any of
their functions under this Part in relation to the
child.

Young people have a right to
contact with their family.

Section 34 (1)

Where a child is in the care of a local authority,
the authority shall (subject to the provisions of
this section) allow the child reasonable contact
with-

(a)   his parents;

(b)   any guardian of his;

(c)   where there was a residential order in force
with respect to this child immediately
before the care order was made, the person
in whose favour the order was made; and

(d)   where, immediately before the care order
was made, a person had care of the child
by virtue of an order made in the exercise
of the High Court's inherent jurisdiction
with respect to children, that person.

Young people can apply to court for the discharge of their care order.

Section 39 (1)

A care order may be discharged by the court on the application of –
(a) any person who has parental responsibility for the child;
(b) the child himself; or
(c) the local authority designated by the order.

Chapter seven
Guidance and regulations

Regulations must be followed by local authorities and other providers of residential services. The regulations which apply to residential care are:

- Children's Homes Regulations 1991
- Arrangement for Placement of Children (General) Regulations 1991
- Review of Children's Cases Regulations 1991
- Contact with Children Regulations 1991
- Representations Procedure (Children) Regulations 1991
- Definition of Independent Visitors (Children) Regulations 1991
- The Children (Secure Accommodation) Regulations 1991
- The Refuges (Children's Homes and Foster Placements) Regulations 1991

All residential social workers should have access to the above regulations which are contained in:

- Children Act Guidance and Regulations Volume 4 Residential Care (yellow book)

which was produced by the Department of Health in 1991.

It is essential that all staff in residential homes have access to Volume 4: **if your home does not have this publication you should request a copy from your line manager immediately.**

What follows is a summary of the regulations in relation to young people's rights. The information is presented in paraphrases rather than direct quotations.

Regulations governing children's residential care

■ Statement of purpose and function

Residential homes should have a written Statement of Purpose and Function which young people can read. This statement will tell young people:
- what help the home will offer them
- how the home is run
- what kind of young people can live in the home
- what happens when young people first go to live at the home
- who the staff who work in the home are (how many; their experience; and their qualifications).

Regulation 4 Children's Homes Reg's 1991

■ Bedrooms

Bedrooms should be suitable to young people's needs and adaptations should be made for disabled young people so that they can 'live as normal a life as possible'.

Regulation 6 Children's Homes Reg's 1991

■ Telephones

In each residential home, there should be a pay telephone where young people can make and receive telephone calls in private.

Regulation 7 (5) Children's Homes Reg's 1991

■ Visitors to homes

There should be space in residential homes for family and friends to visit.

Regulation 7 (3) Children's Homes Reg's 1991

■ Physical condition of homes

Residential homes should have adequate levels of lighting, heating and ventilation and should be 'kept in good structural repair, clean and reasonably decorated and maintained for the care of children.'

Regulation 7 (2) Children's Homes Reg's 1991

■ Prohibited treatment

Young people living in residential care should never be:
- slapped, punched, pushed, roughly handled or have things thrown at them by staff
- refused food or drink
- stopped from seeing their family or friends (unless there are safety risks)
- made to wear clothing which makes them stand out (for example, pyjamas during the day or their shoes taken from them)
- refused medicines or tablets which have been prescribed by a doctor
- deliberately kept awake by staff
- fined by staff.

Regulation 8 (2) Children's Homes Reg's 1991

■ Health

Staff in residential homes should take young people's health seriously and 'ensure that arrangements are made for a child to be provided with health care services, including medical and dental care and treatment'.

Regulation 7 Arrangements for Placement of Children (General) Reg's 1991

Young people should be medically assessed at least once every six months before their second birthday and every year after that.

Regulation 6 Review of Children's Cases Reg's 1991

■ **Education**

Staff in residential homes should take young people's education seriously.

Regulation 4 (1) Arrangements of Placements (general) Reg's 1991

When young people leave school, staff in residential homes should help them arrange their education, employment and training.

Regulation 10 Children's Homes Reg's 1991

■ **Religion**

Young people's religion should be respected and young people should be able 'so far as is practicable, to attend the services of, to receive instruction in, and to observe any requirement (whether as to dress, diet or otherwise)' of their religious persuasion.

Regulation 11 Children's Homes Reg's 1991

■ **Food**

Food in residential homes should be varied and nutritional. Young people of different cultures should be given food that they like and are used to. There should be facilities, as far as is practicable, for young people to prepare their own food if they want.

Regulation 12 Children's Homes Reg's 1991

■ **Clothing**

Young people should be given money to buy clothes.

Regulation 13 Children's Homes Reg's 1991

■ **Written records**

Records written about young people who live in residential care should be kept safe until they are 75 years old.

Regulation 15 (3) Children's Homes Reg's 1991

Regulation 9 Arrangements for Placement for Children (General) Reg's 1991

■ **Monthly visits by external manager**

An external manager should visit each residential home in the local authority every month to check that the home is meeting the needs of young people. She/he should then write a report.

Regulation 22 Children's Homes Reg's 1991

■ **Local authority registration**

Children's homes should be registered by the local authority. During this process the council should state how many young people are permitted to live in the home.

Regulations 25 and 26 Children's Homes Reg's 1991

■ **Local authority visits**

Where a visit has been requested by a voluntary organisation or a manager of a registered children's home, this visit should take place within 14 days.

Where a visit has been requested because a young person might not be safe or well cared for this visit must take place within seven days.

During these visits the young person should be seen alone, reports and papers written by the home must be read and the person visiting must write a report.

Regulation 32 and 34 Children's Homes Reg's 1991

■ **Statutory reviews**

Reviews should be held within four weeks of a young person being looked after.

A second review should be held three months after the first and then every six months.

Regulation 3 Review of Children's Cases Reg's 1991

Young people should, 'unless it is not reasonably practicable', be consulted before their review so that their views can be taken into account during the meeting.

Young people should 'as far as reasonably practicable' be involved in their reviews

Young people should be told the outcome of their reviews.

Regulation 7 Review of Children's Cases Reg's 1991

Review decisions should be recorded in writing.

Regulation 10 Review of Children's Cases Reg's 1991

■ **Contact**

Local authorities can change contact arrangements.

If young people are of sufficient understanding local authorities should obtain their agreement prior to stopping contact.

Regulation 3 Contact with Children Reg's 1991

When a local authority has decided to stop contact between a young person in its care and another person staff must tell the young person if she/he has sufficient understanding.

Regulation 2 Contact with Children Reg's 1991

■ **Complaints**

Where young people make complaints they are entitled to have an independent person involved in the investigation of them.

Regulation 5 Representation Procedure (Children) Reg's 1991

The local authority should investigate and respond to the complaint within 28 days of receiving it.

Regulation 6 (1) Representation Procedure (Children) Regulations 1991

If young people are not happy with the outcome of the complaint they can ask for it to be looked at by a panel of three persons, one of which must be independent of the local authority.

If young people attend a panel they can bring someone to help them.

Regulations 8 representation Procedure (Children) Reg's 1991

■ **Secure accommodation**

A person under 13 years can only be placed in secure accommodation if the Secretary of State agrees.

Regulation 4 The Children (Secure Accommodation) Reg's 1991

A young person cannot be placed in secure accommodation for more than a total of 72 hours during a 28-day period without appearing in court.

Regulation 10 The Children (Secure Accommodation) Reg's 1991

The maximum time a court can say a young person should stay in secure accommodation is three months, unless the young person has been remanded when it can be up to six months.

Regulations 11 and 12 The Children (Secure Accommodation) Reg's 1991

Young people who are remanded in secure accommodation have to return to court every 28 days so that the court can decide whether they should stay in secure accommodation.

Regulation 13 The Children (Secure Accommodation) Reg's 1991

Young people in secure accommodation must be visited by a person who does not work for the local authority within one month of their placement and every three months after that.

Regulation 15 The Children (Secure Accommodation) Reg's 1991

This person should check whether:
- the young person still fits the criteria for being in secure accommodation (see pp. 50–51);
- the placement is suitable;
- there is anywhere else more suitable for the young person.

Regulation 16 The Children (Secure Accommodation) Reg's 1991

Exercise: Implementing the Children Act 1989 regulations

Take each heading from the previous section and indicate how your home implements these regulations.

1 = very good
2 = good
3 = poor
4 = very poor

Heading	Requirement	Rating	What needs to be done
Statement of purpose and function	(1) Home should have a written Statement of Purpose and Function	(1)	
	(2) This Statement should be available to young people who live in the home	(2)	
Bedrooms	(1) Bedrooms should be suitable to young people's needs	(1)	
	(2) Adaptations should be made so that disabled young people can live 'as normal a life as possible'	(2)	
Telephones	There should be a pay telephone in every residential home where young people can make and receive private telephone calls		

This page may be photocopied

Heading	Requirement	Rating	What needs to be done
Visitors to homes	There should be space in every residential home for family and friends to visit		
Physical condition of home	(1) Residential homes should have adequate lighting, heating and ventilation	(1)	
	(2) Homes should be 'kept in good structural repair, clean and reasonably decorated and maintained'	(2)	
Prohibited treatment	Young people who live in residential homes should never be slapped, punched, pushed, roughly handled or have things thrown at them by staff; refused food or drink; stopped from seeing their family or friends (unless there are safety risks); made to wear clothing which makes them stand out; refused medication; deliberately kept awake by staff; fined by staff		
Health	(1) Staff in residential homes need to 'ensure that arrangements are made for a child to be provided with health care services, including medical and dental care and treatment'	(1)	
	(2) Young people over the age of two should be medically assessed every year	(2)	

This page may be photocopied

Heading	Requirement	Rating	What needs to be done
Education	(1) Staff in residential homes should take young people's education seriously	(1)	
	(2) When young people leave school, staff should help them arrange education, employment and training	(2)	
Religion	Young people's religion should be respected and young people should be able to ' so far as is practicable, to attend the services of, to receive instruction in, and to observe any requirement (whether as to dress, diet or otherwise)' of their religious persuasion		
Food	(1) Food in residential homes should be varied and nutritional	(1)	
	(2) Young people from different cultures should be offered food that they like and are used to	(2)	
	(3) There should be facilities for young people to prepare their own food if they want	(3)	
Clothing	Young people should be given money to purchase clothes		

This page may be photocopied

Heading	Requirement	Rating	What needs to be done
Written records	Written records should be kept safe until young people are 75 years old		
Monthly visits by external manager	External managers should make monthly visits to residential homes and write reports about the standard of care within the home		
Local authority registration	(1) Children's homes (for more than three young people) must be registered by local authorities	(1)	
	(2) This registration should state how many young people can live in the home	(2)	
Local authority visits	(1) Where a visit has been requested by a voluntary organisation or a manager of a registered children's home, this visit should take place within 14 days	(1)	
	(2) If a visit has been requested because of concerns about a young person's well-being or care, this must take place within seven days	(2)	

This page may be photocopied

Heading	Requirement	Rating	What needs to be done
Local authority visits (continued)	(3) During these visits the young person must be seen alone, reports and papers written by the home must be read and the person visiting must write a report	(3)	
Statutory reviews	(1) Reviews should be held within one month of a young person first being looked after	(1)	
	(2) A second review should be held three months after the first	(2)	
	(3) Reviews should be six-monthly from then on	(3)	
	(4) Young people should be consulted before their reviews 'unless it is not reasonably practicable'	(4)	
	(5) Young people should be involved in their reviews 'as far as reasonably practicable'	(5)	
	(6) Young people should be told the outcome of their review	(6)	
	(7) Review decisions should be recorded in writing	(7)	
Contact	(1) If a local authority decides to prevent contact between a young person and another person they must inform the young person if she/he has sufficient understanding	(1)	
	(2) If young people have sufficient understanding local authorities should obtain their agreement before preventing contact	(2)	

This page may be photocopied

Heading	Requirement	Rating	What needs to be done
Complaints	(1) When young people make complaints they are entitled to have an independent person involved in the investigation of them	(1)	
	(2) Local authorities should investigate and respond to complaints within 28 days of receiving them	(2)	
	(3) If young people are unhappy with the outcome of their complaint they can ask for it to be considered by a panel	(3)	
	(4) When attending a panel young people can bring someone to help them represent themselves	(4)	
Secure accommodation	(1) A person under 13 years cannot be placed in secure accommodation unless the Secretary of State agrees	(1)	
	(2) A young person cannot be placed in secure accommodation for more than a total of 72 hours within 28 days without appearing in court	(2)	
	(3) The maximum time a court can say a young person can stay in secure accommodation is three months, unless the young person is remanded when it can be up to six months	(3)	
	(4) Young people who are remanded in secure accommodation have to return to court every 28 days so that the court can decide whether they should remain in secure accommodation	(4)	

This page may be photocopied

Heading	Requirement	Rating	What needs to be done
Secure accommodation (continued)	(5) Young people who are placed in secure accommodation must be visited by a person who does not work for the local authority (independent representative) within one month and every three months thereafter	(5)	
	(6) This independent representative should check whether: • the young person still fits the criteria for being in secure accommodation (see pp. 50 – 51) • the placement is appropriate • there is anywhere else more suitable for the young person	(6)	

This page may be photocopied

Chapter eight
Children's rights: current issues and concerns

Have we gone too far with children's rights?

The Children Act 1989 is often regarded as the originator of children's rights. While the Act has significantly improved the rights of young people involved with social services departments, it has had little overall impact on the lives of the 11 million under 18-year-olds in the UK.

When discussing children's rights commentators mistakenly focus on this one piece of legislation. However, its importance dramatically reduces when it is compared to the many other influences affecting young people. A range of individuals and institutions have within their power the means to help or hinder young people express and claim their rights. Parents and school teachers are the two most significant groups of people in the majority of young people's lives. What signs are there to suggest that young people have too many rights within the family, or at school? Parents, for example, are still entitled by law to hit their children (Newell, 1989) and education legislation maintains that the consumers of education are parents, not young people.

For young people's status to significantly improve, change is necessary in all arenas – in the private sphere of the family as well as in public institutions – for example, nurseries, schools, courts and hospitals.

While many adults may feel that children's rights have gone too far, there is little evidence to suggest that this is the case. Take, for instance, the design of buildings and towns and cities – are these accessible to children? If more attention was given to children when designing buildings, wheelchair users would not, for example, have to argue for the lowering of light switches and door handles in public places.

Unfortunately there has been a tendency within the media to exaggerate the negative consequences of promoting children's rights. Concentrating on worst case scenarios, children's rights has been subject to much scare-mongering (Franklin 1995, pp4-5). Teachers' unions, for instance, have vociferously complained about children's rights leading to false allegations against their members (Bennett 1994). Even the radical press has complained that children's rights 'is a nightmare for parents' (Heartfield 1993, p.14).

While research shows us that adults have *always* worried and complained about young people's behaviour (Cohen 1972), and evidence suggests that the number of young people committing offences is decreasing (The Children's Society 1993, p.21-22), the powerful voices of the media and politicians are hard to counter.

Undoubtedly attitudes towards young people have changed and young people's expectations and understanding of their rights have altered. For example, young people in state secondary schools today do not expect to be caned if they misbehave in class (corporal punishment was outlawed in state schools in 1987). More young people living in local authority residential care know that they will not be automatically disbelieved if they complain of mistreatment by adults. This is progress.

It can be very difficult for adults who have experienced a different type of childhood to understand the concerns of children and young people. Once they have passed through childhood themselves, many adults try to forget or romanticise their former experiences. Indeed it is not uncommon for adults to proclaim that excessive cruelty or unjust treatment *did them no harm* (Miller, A. 1987). Because all adults have, by definition, been children it would be fair to expect a special empathy or understanding. Yet as a group of people we display a remarkable capacity for recalling the joys of youth and a conspicuous amnesia for the sadness and pain. Butler and Williamson (1994, p.1) in their research into young people's experience of trauma succinctly explain:

> *any conception of childhood, especially one's own, is constructed, in adulthood, quite differently to how it was experienced at the time.*

Movements for rights for women and black people have caused much conflict for men and white people respectively. Many of the criticisms of children's rights have been levelled at women and black people too. For example:

- *they haven't got the ability to exercise rights*

During the 16th century white colonialists attempted to justify slavery by arguing that African people were sub-human and inferior; a different species from white people. This type of argument was also used against women at the turn of this century – women, it was argued, could not be trusted with the vote because they did not have the ability or constitution required for the harsh world of politics.

- *we have gone too far – they (black people / women / young people) have taken all our rights away*

Popular complaints from men and white people is that they have suffered from the improved status and opportunities gained by women and black people throughout the latter part of this century. Many of these gains are exaggerated.

- *if they want rights they should be prepared to live like us*

White people and men have traditionally held most power in our society. They understand and define the world from this perspective. From their standpoint, it is often assumed that if black people and women want equal status and rights then we must behave like them: there is little room for difference.

'There's not enough rights for everyone!'

Discussions about rights are often based upon the assumption that for some people to gain rights then others must lose theirs. This is not true. Of course there always has to be compromise and negotiation about which rights are to take priority in individual situations. If my neighbour plays loud music in the middle of the night and I need to sleep our rights will clash and one of us will have to compromise. That's life. Why should young people having rights add any special problems? Like adults, they are generally, and to varying degrees, able and willing to negotiate, compromise and give-and-take.

Young people who are empowered by having rights will, however, be more likely to assert themselves and question adults' power. For example:

A residential social worker tells a young person that she cannot have bus fare to visit her mother because he believes that she is going to buy cigarettes with the money.

The young woman becomes angry and states that her care plan says she can have bus fare twice a week and that staff cannot stop her seeing her mum. The member of staff persists, saying that he cannot change the decision which was made in staff changeover. He suggests the young woman waits until the unit manager comes on shift later that afternoon.

The young woman becomes more agitated and says she's going to ring her social worker, or the children's rights officer. Eventually, after kicking the office door for 20 minutes, the young person is given the bus fare but is told that she must bring home the bus tickets because the member of staff still doesn't believe that she will visit her mum. The young woman leaves the building shouting that she is fed up of people thinking that she is a liar.

The above scenario is fairly typical. After the incident the member of staff will probably feel frustrated, demoralised and out of control. He felt he had to carry out instructions but in the end was forced to give in to the young person because a) her care plan said she was entitled to bus fare and b) she was causing too much trouble. What could have been done differently to prevent such a prolonged battle?

Would it have been preferable for the young person to unquestionably accept the decision reached at staff changeover even though she hadn't been involved in making, or agreeing to, it? Was the staff group correct in trying to alter the young woman's care plan in changeover?

It can be very hard to gracefully accept others challenging our power and authority – especially in front of an audience, which is so often the case in residential care. Staff, like young people, have reputations and images to preserve. We live in a society which still ascribes more value to adults' views, opinions and ideas – where young people are not meant to question the word of their elders. It can therefore be quite shocking, even frightening, to be challenged by an individual or group of young people who refuse to obey instructions or orders. It can add insult to injury if these young people then begin to quote the Children Act or threaten to make a complaint. Yet what is the alternative – to expect young people to accept that adults know best even when we do not, or to teach them that their voice should not be heard?

'But what about the staff?'

A residential home for young people is their home – no matter how long or short their period in care or accommodation. However this home is also the workplace of residential workers and it is fair that staff should expect good working conditions and that their employers should take reasonable steps to protect and support them.

Within social work, children's rights has almost become synonymous with complaints: it is no wonder that staff feel frightened and threatened. Complaints procedures are a vital safety-net for young people when other channels of communication have failed. They are not, however, the embodiment of children's rights. Promoting young people's access to complaints is one method of valuing and respecting them; there are many others. Here managers have a crucial role in ensuring that staff understand why it is important that organisations have complaints procedures, and how they can positively affect policies and practice.

If staff are feeling vulnerable and unsupported the solution is not to deny young people their rights. This would be like taking away black people's rights because white people feel uncomfortable or threatened. What is needed is a concerted effort by external managers to genuinely value and appreciate staff. When children's rights advocates meet with residential staff to discuss children's rights it is extremely common to be met with complaints:

- what about *our* rights?
- nobody listens to *us*
- all they're [managers] interested in is filling the beds and keeping to budget
- they [managers] aren't bothered about what we think.

The assumption is that young people are listened to and valued more than staff. Yet comments from young people exactly mirror the complaints of staff! The Children Act 1989 cannot be held responsible for staff not feeling valued by their managers. Reducing the legal entitlements of young people who are looked after will not improve communication between these two groups of professional adults. That is a separate issue which needs to be addressed by the adults concerned.

The successful management of staff is absolutely essential for the promotion of young people's rights in residential care. Staff require, and are entitled to, support and information to carry out their work. For those staff who are used to working in a way which does not promote young people's rights or participation, re-training will be needed so that their social work practice reflects cultural and legal changes. Issuing them with a file of documents saying 'don't do this' or 'you're not allowed to' is certain to have a negative effect. Children's rights will be construed as yet another management device to control and discipline them. In order to promote children's rights and participation positively, it is absolutely essential that staff are confident and clear about what they *can* do to positively care for young people.

The transition of empowering young people in residential care needs to be carefully managed and the needs and rights of staff should not be forgotten. Otherwise the concept and everyday practice of children's rights will be seen as a threat by the very people whose primary function is to protect and promote the rights of young people.

Mixed messages

Within social services' settings, messages about the importance of children's rights are ambiguous. On the one hand, the requirements of the Children Act 1989 and the United Nations Convention on the Rights of the Child emphasise the need to involve young people in decision-making and gives special responsibility to staff for assisting young people to participate and make choices. Yet staff and young people are not immune to the current antipathy, even hostility, towards young people – in local communities, the media and political parties.

The law demands that young people who live in residential care are treated as individuals with certain rights and entitlements, yet there exists a gut resistance among many adults towards children's rights. This duplicity can cause real confusion, especially for those adults who are parents.

'If it's good enough for my son or daughter, why not for others?'

At home a residential social worker can prevent a son or daughter leaving the house at midnight, stop pocket money allowances indefinitely and even lawfully hit her/him. Yet these courses of action would be open to question and criticism at work.

Staff who work in residential care have clear professional roles and responsibilities towards young people, prescribed and informed by legislation and government guidance. Kahan explains in her introduction to *Growing Up in Groups* (1994, p.4) how:

The care aspect of group living is greatly underestimated and under-valued, unlike special skills associated with it like medicine and teaching. This is, perhaps, because it is often regarded as an extension of ordinary childrearing which has traditionally been undervalued and taken for granted.

Professionally caring for people is a complex and demanding job. Genuine care and respect can only be partially taught but these personal attributes can, however, be nurtured by good training and management support. There are many tools and skills particular to residential work and looking after young people – for example communication skills, helping young people cope with loss and groupwork methods – which need to be learned and developed. Being a parent may bring lots of advantages to working with young people – for example, increased confidence and knowledge of child development – but it does not guarantee success!

There are many features of group living which small families of four or five people do not have to contend with. Ensuring that everyone has a say and gets involved in decision-making grows more difficult as the numbers of people increase. Add to this the fact that in residential care people are often unrelated, of varying ages and abilities, have divergent needs and belong to a range of ethnic groups. Some people may not want to be in the home (young people or staff) and there may be structural factors inhibiting participation – for example in secure units where young people's mobility outside of the home is restricted. Despite all this there *are* many ways of promoting young people's rights and encouraging participation in residential care.

'Can young people have rights without responsibilities?'

Over the last decade a particular view of rights has developed within social policy: that individual rights must be tied with responsibilities.

Within, for example, the national health service people who have not demonstrated personal responsibility – for instance heavy smokers with heart disease – have in some cases had health care refused. Their rights to free health care have been reduced because of their behaviour.

Similar developments have occurred in social security where claimants must demonstrate responsibility by actively seeking employment. In the area of public housing there has been focus in recent years upon the assumed fecklessness of single mothers and questions about their entitlement to council housing priority have been raised.

This assumption – that you cannot have rights unless you accept and demonstrate responsibility – has also spread within social services, particularly in children's residential care.

It is not uncommon to hear that young people in residential care have rights *and* responsibilities. For example, many charters of rights and responsibilities have been produced.

A recent Support Force publication, *Good Care Matters* (1995b, pp.97-99) stresses the link between rights and responsibilities. In a very helpful section on rights and responsibilities, the following is stressed:

> *From the point of view of developing children and young people, they have two main lessons to learn:*
>
> – *they have rights but they also have responsibilities*
>
> – *they must respect the rights and responsibilities of others, both peers and staff.*

Few people would disagree with the above – there is nothing controversial about believing that we all have responsibilities towards other people. However, great problems can arise from linking rights and responsibilities – essentially this pairing can lead to the mistaken belief that irresponsible behaviour can lead to the wholesale removal of rights.

If we understand children's rights to mean that

i)   we value and respect young people as human beings and

ii) young people have certain legal entitlements

it is difficult to accept that all rights are conditional on behaviour.

Rights as human beings

Arguably, there are basic rights which all human beings have. Given that these are universal rights, they should never be taken away from young people who live in residential care:

- right to respect
- right to dignity
- right to fair treatment.

Legal rights

Some legal rights within residential care can *never* be taken away – no matter how young people behave. These include:

- food
- shelter
- warmth
- clothing
- protection from abuse
- legal representation
- access to complaints procedures.

Other rights can *only* be removed through civil, criminal or administrative proceedings. These include:

- consultation and involvement in decision-making forums (planning meetings and reviews; case conferences)
- access to information (in files, records and reports)
- liberty and mobility
- contact with family.

Many rights will be subject to negotiation and compromise and will be linked to young people's behaviour. For example:

- a young person's right to receive pocket money may be affected by whether or not she/he has to contribute to the cost of repairing something she/he has deliberately broken;
- a young person's rights to free expression will be subject to rules about not harming or hurting others (for example, not being racist or criticising other young people's families).

'Why all this focus on responsibilities?'

There are several possible reasons to explain why personal responsibility has become a fashionable concept in recent years.

(i) Resources

Where individual responsibility has been stressed in other areas of welfare, this has occurred against a backdrop of stretched resources and growing demand for services. Rationing is a device used to allocate scarce resources. The numbers of people entitled to social security, housing and health care has been affected by demographic changes (particularly in the growing population of older people), social and economic conditions and increased expectations. In order to curb demand and spending, new rules have been introduced. Many of these focus on the behaviour of people who use welfare be they unemployed, unmarried mothers or homeless people.

(ii) Caring for young people

Staff who look after young people in residential care want to make sure that they respect other people. This is an indisputable task of any parent or person in a parental role. Promoting responsibility is extremely important and being responsible is a positive quality which staff try very hard to engender in young people. However, by linking responsibility to the threat of losing rights this may actually reverse its importance and value – basically responsibility is being promoted in a negative way.

(iii) Views about young people

How many social services departments have developed charters of rights and responsibilities for older people?

It sometimes seems that staff and managers in social services departments feel more comfortable or willing to link rights and responsibilities when talking about young people. Why is this?

One reason may be that young people are still growing and need help and guidance. But surely this can be given alongside the strong message that they have rights. Young people need to be aware of the consequences of their actions but this message does not have to be shrouded in threats about losing rights.

It is also unfair to demand that young people exercise responsibility in the same way as adults when they do not have the powers that we have. For example, economic independence or rights to move, to leave school, get a job or vote in national or local government elections. So the question could also be asked: can young people have responsibilities without powers?

'Promoting children's rights: what can I do?'

As a general rule adults have more power and status in our society than young people. Any adult who is committed to children's rights must question her/his own behaviour and attitudes:

- how do I benefit from young people's dependency upon me?
- do I expect young people to respect and listen to me just because I am older?
- does being around young people make me feel bigger/stronger/more knowledgeable?
- do I listen to and value the views of adults more than young people?
- when I'm with young people, how often do I say sorry or admit I'm wrong?
- what do I enjoy about being with young people?
- how much power am I prepared to give up?
- in what ways do I encourage young people to make decisions and assert themselves?

As well as questioning our beliefs, assumptions about and attitudes towards young people, as adults, we need to assess our current knowledge about their lives and experiences. Butler and Williamson explain that:

the social world inhabited by children is different from that experienced by an older generation, and adults must be humble enough to acknowledge this and inquisitive enough to be willing to learn about it (1994, p.86)

- how much do we know about the laws which affect young people's lives?
- what does it feel like to be young in the 1990s?
- how does impairment affect young people's experience of childhood: in what ways are they disabled by their environment and society generally?
- what is it like to belong to a minority community – for example: what are black young people's experiences; how does it feel to be lesbian, gay or bisexual; what is it like being in care or accommodation?
- how much do we know about youth culture – music, sport and pop

personalities, fashion, language, politics, games and other leisure activities?

'Who makes the rules round here?'

Developing a culture in a residential home which respects young people's rights as individuals will require an on-going appraisal of rules and routines. When a young person or new member of staff first enters a residential home she/he will spend the first couple of weeks figuring out the rules, and trying to work out who is in charge. Frequently she/he will then begin to ask questions: to her/him things that others take for granted may appear strange or unnecessary, even stupid.

Some of the questions people new to a residential home might ask include:

Why do young people have to be down for breakfast by 10am on weekends?

Who decided that young people's friends can only visit on Wednesdays?

Why are there no pets allowed in this home?

When do you decide young people's bedtimes?

Why do young people have to put their laundry outside their bedroom doors on Monday mornings?

Who decided that supper is at 7pm every night?

When did you last discuss the layout of the furniture in the lounge?

Why are young people not involved in selecting new members of staff?

Who decided that young people shouldn't watch television in their pyjamas or night-dresses?

How these enquiries are received will indicate how open staff and managers are to being challenged – as individuals and as members of a group.

The absence of challenges may show that everyone is happy with the rules and routines of the home. Alternatively it may show that people are too frightened to speak out – or that they don't think their opinions will count.

When were the rules and routines last questioned in your home? Who made the challenge? How was it received?

Chapter nine
Participation in residential care

Defining participation

Participation means being involved or taking part. It can refer to:

(i)   individuals making decisions about their own lives

(ii)   groups of people taking action and making decisions together

(iii) members of a community taking part in an activity or project with a common purpose.

Ladder of citizen participation

In 1971 Sherry Arnstein wrote an influential article about citizen participation in public planning schemes. Her ladder of citizen participation remains a very popular and useful tool. There are eight rungs on Arnstein's ladder ranging from manipulation to citizen control:

Rung	Type of participation	Characteristics
Eighth rung	citizen control	citizens have control of resources and are able to manage projects without interference or strings attached
Seventh rung	delegated power	citizens have significant control of resources and have a real say. Where views differ, 'bargaining' takes place rather than officials having the power to decide
Sixth rung	partnership	planning and decision-making responsibilities shared

(Continued on next page.)

Fifth rung	placation	some degree of influence but tokenism still evident
Fourth rung	consultation	citizens are given information (if consultation not paired with other methods of participation Arnstein believes 'this rung of the ladder is still a sham')
Third rung	information	one-way information from officials to citizens
Second rung	therapy	emphasis upon curing or treating citizens – for example self-help groups set up by official bodies
Bottom rung	manipulation	using citizens to 'rubber-stamp' decisions or increase reputation of officials. Arnstein labels this type of participation 'a Mickey Mouse game'

An adaptation of Arnstein's ladder was produced by Roger Hart in 1992. His ladder specifically relates to young people's participation. What follows is an attempt to further modify Arnstein's typology to relate to residential care.

Table 5: Ladder of young people's participation in residential care

Rung	Example in residential care	Characteristics
eighth rung – citizen control	young people are allowed to choose how to decorate their bedrooms and are given money to buy materials	real choice and control over resources
seventh rung – delegated power	young people are encouraged to make decisions about how to spend home's activity budget	real choice within clearly defined boundary
sixth rung – partnership	young people are involved in the recruitment and selection of staff	genuine partnership between managers and young people each party has equal say in decision
fifth rung – placation	young people are asked to produce menu-plans by copying out meals already decided by staff	illusion of participation but no real decision-making involved
fourth rung – consultation	when inspectors visit, young people are asked about the home but they are not given feedback	information obtained from young people but no effort made to explain how and if they have affected future practice and policies
third rung – information	young people are given a list of the rules of their home	information given with no scope for negotiation or discussion
second rung – therapy	young people are encouraged to meet as a group *only* when there are problems between them – for example, bullying	participation and involvement only encouraged when it helps staff control young people's behaviour
bottom rung – manipulation	young people are visited by a senior manager who asks them what they think about a recent decision to close their home	tokenistic exercise which does not allow young people to influence or change decision

When discussing young people's participation in residential care it is necessary to address two fundamental questions. First, do young people have the ability or competence to make decisions and participate? Second, what are the benefits of promoting participation in residential homes?

'Let them be children: decisions are for adults'

Adults often feel that they have to protect young people from having to make too many decisions. Childhood is seen as a precious time where young people should not be burdened with adult decision-making. This approach often masks the very real decisions which young people do make, and denies the competencies and skills which are evident in very young people:

> *Decision-making is often seen as purely adult behaviour, because adults control most of the resources over which choices are made. By observing and talking to children, however, it is clear that learning to choose and decide starts very early, from a choice whether to play with one toy or another, to choosing where to sit on the top of a bus, etc. The options increase with the child's mobility and the willingness of adults to open up new areas of choice and possible risk*

(Ruth Gardner in *Who Says? Choice and Control in Care* 1987, p.23-4)

The types of decisions young people make will change and vary as they develop and grow. If we examine closely some of the experiences which young people live through – sometimes without close support from a trusted adult – we can see that they are able to exercise choice and make rational decisions.

During interviews with 190 young people, aged between six and 17 years, in nine local authority children's homes, four secondary schools, two junior schools and two youth clubs, Butler and Williamson (1994) learnt about a range of childhood experiences which worried or frightened young people. These included:

- abuse and neglect
- adoption
- being admitted to foster or residential care
- bullying
- changing school
- death of family member
- domestic violence
- drug-dependent parents
- name-calling
- parental arguments and divorce and separation
- parental mental illness

- pregnancy
- rape and murder

Only one of the sample reported that she worried about nothing.

Upon further investigation the researchers found that many of the young people they interviewed preferred not to talk with adults about their fears. One 13-year-old boy commented that ' ... *you have to find ways of dealing with things yourself. No-one else can do it for you.*' (p.75).

While this research gives clear messages to adults – particularly those who professionally care for young people – about the need to be more receptive to young people, there is a powerful undercurrent about young people's resilience, capabilities and their strong desire to be involved and valued. The consequences of denying young people's involvement can be disastrous:

> *I never saw my mum in hospital after my dad attacked her. I didn't go to the funeral. I don't even know where her grave is. Nobody told me anything, probably because they thought I was too young. But nobody even tried. And I can't ask now 'cos all the staff that were here then have moved on. But that was actually worse than my mum actually dying.*

> (17-year-old young woman quoted in Butler and Williamson 1994, p.52)

People who proclaim that young people have not the competence or ability to make decisions are frequently underestimating the value of experience in acquiring skills and confidence. As Franklin (1995, p.11) argues:

> *If children are not allowed to make decisions because they have no experience of decision making, how do they ever get started? This is Catch 22*

A self-fulfilling prophecy can result from not allowing young people the chance to make decisions:

- adults believe young people cannot make decisions
- we therefore do not help or allow them to make decisions
- young people do not have the skills or confidence to make decisions
- we were right: young people cannot make decisions.

'But it's harder in a home'

Within residential care individual decision-making can be restricted by the rules and routines of homes. These rules may have developed as a consequence of trying to accommodate the needs of all young people who live in a home. Conversely, they may have been introduced to make life easier for staff, managers or the organisation generally.

A fairly ordinary day

Every day adults make a series of often taken-for-granted decisions, starting with when to get out of bed and ending with choosing what time to go to bed. These decisions will include:

- what time to get up;

- how to get up – for example lie in bed for 15 minutes after alarm clock has gone off, or rise immediately;

- whether to shower or have a bath;

- what to wear;

- what to have for breakfast;

- what time to leave the house if in employment;

- which colleagues to talk to, or confide in, at work;

- what to eat for lunch;

- after leaving work, choices are made about how to spend the evening – perhaps it will be spent sharing a takeaway family meal, or watching television. Something may have planned in advance or a decision taken spontaneously;

- when to go to bed – including whether to read for a while or watch television or play music;

- finally when to turn the bedroom light off.

Of course none of us makes choices without considering the effect upon others. We all have constraints on our personal freedom. If we live with other people, our decisions will have to take them into account. We may have responsibility for caring for other people – for example, a child or an older relative. Obviously income will significantly affect choices and many decisions will require understanding and experience which we may not have. Additionally, decisions and choices may be restricted because of the design and layout of the physical environment.

'What are the benefits of participation?'

The process of young people making decisions and getting involved in running their home is not easy – for young people or staff, particularly if the culture of the home has previously discouraged participation. Each party may:

- feel vulnerable and unsure
- fear looking stupid or making mistakes
- require support and encouragement.

Despite the obvious difficulties, there are real benefits to encouraging young people's participation. These can be divided into benefits to individuals and to organisations.

Benefits to individuals	Benefits to organisations
• feel valued and important;	• people who feel valued are more likely to behave well;
• improve and develop skills;	• learning and sharing of experiences is fostered;
• increased knowledge;	
• more opportunities to meet people;	• encourages working and living together cooperatively;
• more opportunities to develop relationships and make friends.	• increased skills and confidence;
	• people who have been involved in reaching decisions (for example, in a review, staff meeting or supervision session) are more likely to adhere to what was agreed.

'Why is participation so important?'

To find out why it is important for young people to participate it is helpful to first consider why participation is important to us.

How many times have people made decisions without talking with you first, even though you are affected? This may have been in your family, at school, at work or in your local neighbourhood.

- How would you feel if you went home tonight and found that your bedroom had been moved to another room? What if your neighbour had erected a fence around your garden or painted your front door? How about if the council had decided to place a recycling centre at the bottom of your road? What if you come into work tomorrow to find that you have been transferred to another community home?

- If people around you continually did things without asking you what would this tell you about what they think of you? Would you feel that they respect and value you, that they are interested in your opinions? Would you feel important? Or would you think people thought you were stupid or unimportant?
(Continued on next page.)

Exercise: Remembering how I used to feel

What decisions did you make at home?

- Did you live in a family where adults always made the decisions?

- Were discussions encouraged in your family?

- Did everyone get a chance to have their say?

What decisions did you make at school?

- Did your teachers encourage you to get involved in your school?

- Were the rules at your school made by teachers *and* young people?

- Can you think of any times when decisions were made about you without you being involved? How did this make you feel?

A familiar compliment young people make about adults who listen to them is: *'she/he doesn't treat me like a child'*
Roughly translated this often means that the adult has taken them seriously and has encouraged, rather than discouraged, their involvement in an activity, discussion or event.

Exercise: Some benefits of participation in groups or organisations

① List the groups or organisations that you are a member of

_____

_____

_____

_____

_____

② What skills have you developed through being a member of these groups or organisations?

_____

_____

_____

_____

_____

③ List the groups or organisations which young people you work with participate in

_____

_____

_____

_____

_____

④ What skills have young people developed as a consequence of being a member of these groups or organisations?

_____

_____

_____

_____

_____

How do YOU encourage the young people you look after to get involved in groups or organisations outside your home?

This page may be photocopied

Exercise: Obstacles to participation

Think of a recent situation at work where you were not able to express yourself as well as you wanted. Perhaps this was in a young person's review, in supervision or a staff meeting.

I didn't say what I wanted to in

_____

The reasons for this include _____

_____

_____

_____

It would have been easier for me if _____

_____

_____

_____

To have my say the next time, I need to _____

_____

_____

_____

To have my say next time other people will need to _____

_____

_____

How do YOU affect young people's participation?

This page may be photocopied

Some examples of participation

Individual decision-making	Group participation	Community participation
Making choices about where and with whom we live	People coming together to provide services to others (school governors; voluntary groups; hospital visiting schemes; prison visitors)	People in a locality coming together to campaign for a local resource (pedestrian crossing; prevent closure of local school; play facilities; improved housing)
Looking after our health		
Deciding when and what to eat	People coming together to share a particular leisure activity (leisure groups; Brownies and Cubs; newsletter or magazine groups in schools)	People in a locality coming together to develop and run a local resource (toddler group; cooperative food store; youth club; neighbourhood watch scheme)
Choosing clothes		
Making friends		
Choosing layout and decoration of home		
Deciding how to spend the day	Users of local authority and health services coming together to support each other (disability advocacy groups; young people's in-care groups; school councils; support groups for parents of disabled people; black young people's in-care groups; lesbian and gay groups; women's groups)	People with specific religious beliefs coming together to provide services to others (Sunday schools; youth clubs; meals to homeless and poor people; financial assistance)
Planning education, training and employment		
Developing political and/or religious beliefs		
Planning holidays		People from specific ethnic groups coming together to provide services to themselves and others (Saturday and supplementary schools; residential homes; women's groups; arts and cultural centres; welfare rights advice; support groups for people surviving racial attacks)
Making long-term life plans		
	People coming together to campaign for improvements in work conditions (trade unions; women's groups; black workers' groups; lesbian and gay groups)	
		People who belong to a community based on age, gender, class or other characteristic coming together to provide services to themselves and others (women's centres; unemployed worker's groups or clubs; in-care groups)
		People coming together to represent and take political action with others (politicians; community activists)

Participation in residential care

In a residential setting there are many activities which young people can participate in. These relate to young people being actively involved in decisions about their own lives, their residential home and policies and practice generally. Young people will rarely make these decisions alone or unaided – usually they will require help from others.

Individual decision-making	Group level participation	Community level participation
Where they are going to live	Making decisions about interior and exterior furnishings	Membership of local in-care group
Who they are going to live with		Influencing allocation of resources across services for young people and their families
Decisions about education and hopes for the future	Making decisions about: bed-times; pocket money and other allowances; when and where visitors can stay	
Decisions about looking after their health		Influencing the design and layout of newly built homes
Choice of friends, clothing, bedroom furnishings	Choice of food and decisions about activities and holidays	Membership on council committees and departmental working groups
Decisions about contact with members of family and local community	Influencing and being involved in the recruitment and selection of staff	Involvement in the local authority inspection of homes, including producing standards for residential homes
Membership of local youth club or involvement in other groups	Being involved in carrying out household chores and tasks (including preparation and cooking of meals)	
Choice of religion and political beliefs		Membership on Inspection Advisory Panels
Choice of partner and decisions about sexual relationships	Making decisions about form of transport used by home	
	Making decisions about how different behaviour should be responded to by young people and staff (for example: racism; bullying; smoking in communal spaces)	
	Involvement in the preparation of Statement of Purpose and Function of homes	

Encouraging participation in residential care: physical environment

The physical environment of a residential home symbolises how much young people are valued. If young people do not feel that they are valued – or that their home matters – it will be very difficult to generate interest in participation. A recent Support Force publication (1995b, p.37) explains:

> *By providing a quality environment, staff are effectively saying "We value you enough to provide this. Now you value yourself in the same way ..." When the physical environment is treated with respect, it becomes something from which those who live and work in it gain self-respect.*

(i) Signs outside residential homes

A large sign outside a home may help visitors find their way but it is also likely to embarrass young people who live in the home

- many signs have been removed from outside residential homes.

(ii) How homes are referred to

When young people have to give the name of their home rather than an address their care status immediately becomes public. There are many instances where they will need to give their address – for example: when they are at school; while filling in application forms for college courses and employment; if they are registering with a general practitioner or being admitted to hospital. To avoid stigma it is therefore preferable to use addresses rather than names.

- some local authorities have decided to stop giving residential homes names and refer instead to addresses.

(iii) Gardens

Gardens say a lot about the care and respect given to the interior of homes. Gardens are the first thing young people and visitors see.

- staff and young people can be encouraged to help to take care of the home's garden/s.

(iv) Paintwork

Front doors which have been scratched or covered in graffiti by previous residents can give a very bad impression of the home.

Paintwork on the outside of buildings says a lot about how much value is placed on the people who live and work in the building.

- regular painting of front door ensures that scratches and graffiti do not become acceptable features of residential homes
- regular painting of exterior of home shows people who live and work in the home that they are valued.

(v) Condition and style of front door, entrance and reception area

A front door is one of the first things young people see when they enter a home. Heavy doors can be difficult for young children and people with physical impairments to open.

What does your front door say about your home? Is it indistinguishable from other houses in your neighbourhood? Has it a number?

If a front door leads to a waiting area and general reception, what kinds of things welcome young people?

- most community homes take special care to make the front door and entrance area to homes welcoming and pleasant. Some examples include: plants; welcome mat; brightly painted front door; light outside door (particularly important for young people who enter the home in the middle of the night);
- many residential homes have made substantial improvements to waiting and reception areas over the last few years. These include plants; pleasant pictures; comics, children's books and toys and magazines; comfortable seats; and friendly reception staff. Reception staff are extremely important as they can be the first adults in the home which young people meet. If they are friendly, interested and helpful this can be a very good start for young people;
- some local authorities have placed brass or metal number plates on all doors of community homes (while this is less institutional it also reminds people to use the full address of the home).

(vi) Condition of windows

Windows and curtains or blinds which are dirty or damaged give the impression that the people who live and work in the home are not valued. They can also give the message to the surrounding community that people who live in the home are dirty.

Some homes have had to put bars on windows in order to prevent young people falling or jumping out and hurting themselves. There are a whole range of bars which can be placed on windows – from those used in prisons and police-cells to those used on domestic properties. If your home has bars on the windows, what messages do they give to young people and the surrounding community?

- most residential homes view the cleaning of windows and curtains or blinds as being of equal importance to other cleaning;
- many residential homes have purchased very discreet or decorative window bars. The result is that the home does not appear prison-like.

(vii) Choice and layout of furniture in homes

Furniture that is institutional or is in a bad state of repair conveys a lack of respect to people who live and work in residential homes. Heavy wear and tear is to be expected in residential homes: the physical environment is an integral part of the service to young people and should be maintained on a par with other aspects of residential care.

Homes where disabled young people live need to be fully accessible in order to encourage their mobility and independence.

If young people are given opportunities to choose furniture they are more likely to have respect for their surroundings. They will also feel valued and important.

- young people can be encouraged to choose furniture. They can accompany staff when shopping and look through brochures and catalogues. Group discussions can be facilitated to ascertain young people's preferences. *This obviously means that central purchasing is to be avoided wherever possible*;
- homes where disabled young people live can be purpose-built or adapted to ensure that, for example: surfaces are of varying heights;

door widths are big enough for wheelchairs; handles and door-knobs are within reach; cupboards and their contents are accessible;

- young people can be involved in deciding the layout of furniture in different rooms. If there is a particular room in the home where reviews and planning meetings are held, it is important that young people are encouraged to help make this room as comfortable as possible – they could, for example, be asked what pictures or plants to put in this room: some young people may enjoy taking special responsibility for maintaining and looking after the room.

(viii)   Choice of wall coverings (communal areas and private rooms)

Wall coverings which are institutional (for example, homes which are painted the same colour throughout) or in a bad state of repair convey a lack of respect and value to the people who live and work in the home. Encouraging young people to become involved in choosing wall coverings will assist them in developing a sense of pride and value in their surroundings.

- young people can be encouraged to become involved in choosing communal wall coverings. They may also help with the painting and decorating if they want to;
- young people, particularly those living in long-stay homes, can be encouraged to choose the colour of paint and style of wallpaper for their bedroom. They can also help with painting and decorating.

(ix)   Personal items

If all property within homes is viewed as belonging to the council personal pride and responsibility will be difficult to engender. People generally value things they see as their own or which they have a stake in:

- many residential homes actively encourage young people to purchase their own toiletries;
- many residential homes encourage young people to choose and purchase their own mugs, towels and particular items of bedroom furniture;
- many residential homes actively encourage, and provide money for, young people to regularly buy their own comics, newspapers and magazines;
- most residential homes will invite young people to choose a favourite

photograph of themselves or their family to place in a communal area, alongside other photographs.

(x) Office

The type, location and purpose of the office is important in a number of ways:

(i)   if staff spend most, or a large proportion, of their time in the office this means that young people are not being given the care and attention they should have;

(ii) if the office is located in the middle of a home this can exaggerate its importance, making it a focal point when it should be a minor feature of the home;

(iii) if young people are not allowed in the office this can nurture and exacerbate a culture of 'us and them'. This in turn may provoke situations where young people have to misbehave to get into the office and receive adult attention;

(iv) in some homes the office has become the place where young people are taken to 'cool off' or be restrained. This can reinforce ideas of it being one of the most significant and important places in the home. Mystique can also develop about what happens to young people in the office.

- Some residential homes do not have a designated office;
- many homes have deliberately located offices away from the main rooms in order to lessen their significance;
- many homes have made the smallest room in the house the office – this has the effect of minimising the room's importance;
- many staff encourage young people to sit with them while they are writing daily logs or reports which concern that individual young person. Similarly many homes take active steps to prevent the office being either the main site of conflict or activity – basically by avoiding, whenever possible, staff grouping in this room;
- staff can carry out many administrative tasks when they are with young people – in the lounge and other communal rooms for example.

Encouraging participation in residential care: staff group

Residential work involves staff working as a team. It is therefore crucial that staff see that their individual efforts have a common purpose. Achieving positive outcomes for young people will be difficult if staff are unclear about what they are doing and why (Parker and others, 1991).

Staff who disagree with the work and values of colleagues can be tempted to undermine their work. This is especially relevant when changes are occurring – particularly within the area of children's rights and participation. Open and honest communication is a necessary pre-condition of working as part of a residential team.

Where there is little cohesion, common purpose or solidarity between staff this can lead to them feeling powerless and insignificant as individuals.

Young people who live in residential homes need to know that the adults who care for them have a common purpose. Insecurity and fear can result from living in a home where staff have no shared objectives and work as individuals rather than as a team. Young people are also well able to spot divisions and weaknesses in a staff group. These divisions can be exploited if staff do not work together.

- Many homes organise regular meetings and events where staff can come together to share their ideas and positively plan their work;
- some local authorities actively encourage the involvement of staff in the preparation of individual Statements of Purpose and Function;
- staff supervision and meetings often address issues about team-work;
- special iniatives to develop the awareness and practice of residential staff have been developed by the National Children's Bureau Children's Residential Care Unit and the National Institute for Social Work for example.

Encouraging participation in residential care: home managers

The head of home is the biggest single influence upon it: in some cases, a determining influence upon its culture, ethos and practice.

(Sir William Utting in *Children in the Public Care* 1991, p.13)

Managers of residential establishments have considerable power and influence. Their attitudes, values and leadership styles make a great difference to the culture and running of a home. Managers who do not value or welcome the experience and skills of their staff will certainly have difficulty accepting the experiences and skills of young people.

The extent of managers' commitment to children's rights and participation will significantly influence developments within homes. Managers, like staff, can undermine children's rights and participation. Often this can be based upon fear of losing control and an unwillingness to lose or share power.

Making changes in any group or organisation is hard work! Managers who want to bring about positive change need to have energy, creativity and ideas. If the changes are against the present culture of the organisation they may also have to endure criticism, scapegoating and sabotage.

- Many managers of residential homes actively encourage open and honest dialogue between young people, staff and themselves;
- during supervision managers can ensure that the strengths and abilities of their staff are recognised (Support Force for Children's Residential Care 1995c);
- regular staff meetings will give managers the opportunity to encourage the development of good practice;
- many managers make a point of spending regular time with young people in their home. Similarly, many have developed and encouraged an 'open door' policy where young people in their home can approach them to discuss not only problems but also their ideas for developing their home.

Encouraging participation in residential care: external managers

Many problems in children's homes in the past have occurred because managers and elected bodies have failed to take their responsibilities seriously enough, or arrangements for monitoring and oversight have been inadequate.

(Barbara Kahan in *Growing Up in Groups* 1994, p.280)

External line managers have a key role in ensuring that young people are involved in the running of their home, and in making decisions about their own lives. The messages they communicate to staff and managers about young people's rights and participation will influence expectations and practice. Inaction on the part of external managers gives a clear signal that participation is not a priority.

- Young people's participation can be discussed and monitored during supervision with unit or home managers;
- external managers can ensure that young people know who they are, and feel able to approach them;
- meetings with unit or home managers can address practice issues relating to participation where homes can share experiences and learn from each other;
- external managers can ensure that staff and managers receive up-to-date information relating to legislation, research and good practice material;
- external managers can initiate special projects to find out what young people in residential care collectively feel about services. Nottinghamshire and Hampshire social services departments have undertaken such initiatives;
- when producing information for children's services plans, and planning services generally, managers can actively promote and support consultation with young people (Dartington Social Research Unit 1995).

Encouraging participation in residential care: reviews

> *... the social worker and staff will not consult the children. If they could just sit down and talk it over with us, they could come to much better conclusions than thinking for us and putting down a conclusion we might not like. After all it's our life and our future that's being decided*

(young person cited in Page and Clark 1977, p.31)

> *I never have the courage to talk because I am alone in a room with about five types of social worker. When I speak, everyone doesn't listen*

(young person cited in Fletcher 1993, p.57)

Young people's participation in reviews requires particular attention because these meetings affect their lives enormously. Reviews are especially important for they can determine:

- where a young person lives
- who a young person lives with
- who a young person has contact with
- what type of education a young person should receive

- the medical and health care needs of a young person
- whether an independent visitor should be appointed
- whether adoption proceedings should be pursued
- whether an application is to be made for a secure accommodation order

These decisions have great impact on the lives and well-being of young people yet research continues to suggest that young people do not feel included in making or agreeing these important life plans. The recently launched Department of Health *Looking After Children* initiative should help staff focus on all aspects of young people's needs and developmental milestones. The Department of Health's expectation is that young people will be fully involved in completing their *assessment and action records* and in their reviews. There are a number of ways in which residential homes can address and improve young people's participation in reviews.

- Staff in homes can facilitate group discussions and practice sessions on reviews among young people. Children's rights officers and staff who chair reviews can be invited to run these sessions if residential staff do not feel equipped or confident; the independence of children's rights officers and review chairpersons may also prove useful to young people;
- linkworkers and keyworkers can ensure that young people are consulted about where and when their review is to be held, and who should be invited. Linkworkers and keyworkers can also check whether young people want an advocate, friend or a favourite relative to attend the meeting to support them. Special time can be set aside for young people and their keyworkers to prepare for their forthcoming review: the recent guide produced by Wheal and Sinclair (1995) should prove particularly useful in this one-to-one setting;
- information about the importance and purpose of reviews should be included in any written documents given to young people when they enter residential care;
- special training can be arranged for residential staff in order that they understand the child care planning process and the role of reviews within this. Given that many linkworkers or keyworkers act as young people's advocates (someone who speaks up for them), it is crucial that they are confident within this type of setting and are able to articulate the young person's needs and wishes clearly;
- residential staff and managers can try helping young people express themselves in meetings by using videos, tape-recordings and drawings and poems for example. For young people who are unable, or do not

have the confidence, to record their views in writing, speaking into a tape-recorder or drawing a picture to show their plans and hopes for the future can access much information previously out of reach. Similarly preparing a short ten-minute video about how their life is, and what they want for the future, can relieve the dullness and boredom which young people often associate with meetings;

- training for staff who chair reviews needs to incorporate the views and suggestions of young people;
- checklists can be produced to help residential staff prepare themselves and young people for reviews. An example of what may be included in such a checklist is on page 100;
- other checklists can be produced to help residential staff increase young people's participation during reviews. Examples of what could be included are on pages 101 and 102.

Table 6: Checklist for young people's participation in reviews

This form is to be completed by linkworker/keyworker at least one week before review

Name of young person . . . .

Date of birth . . . .

Date and time of last review . . . .

Date and time of this review . . . .

Has the young person been involved in deciding:

where review is to be held	YES/NO
when review is to be held	YES/NO
who is invited to review	YES/NO
the agenda for meeting	YES/NO

Has the young person read reports written by:

residential staff	YES/NO
field social worker	YES/NO
education staff	YES/NO
psychologist or psychiatrist	YES/NO
anyone else	YES/NO

Has the young person made comments on any of these reports?   YES/NO

Who is responsible for bringing these comments to meeting?

. . . .

Has the young person participated in group session on reviews within residential home?   YES/NO

Has the young person had some special time with her/his linkworker or social worker to prepare for review?   YES/NO

If yes, please state when and for how long (eg 22 April: two hours)

. . . .

If no, please state why

. . . .

Has the young person prepared a report, video, tape-recording or any other material for review?   YES/NO

If yes, who will ensure that this is brought to the meeting?   YES/NO

. . . .

If no, please explain why

. . . .

Does the young person want to bring anything else to the meeting (for example, a school report or sports award)?   YES/NO

If yes, who will ensure that this is brought to the meeting? . . . .

Does the young person want a special friend, advocate or relative to attend the review?   YES/NO

If yes, who will ensure this person is invited?

. . . .

Does the young person need collecting from school/college/work to attend the review?   YES/NO

If yes, who will collect her/him?

. . . .

Will the young person require a snack or meal before the review?   YES/NO

If yes, who will ensure this is prepared?

. . . .

Name of linkworker/keyworker . . . .

Date form completed . . . .

Signature of young person . . . .

Signature of staff member . . . .

Table 7: Example checklist for young people's participation in reviews

During a review

1. Has the young person:
    - a comfortable seat?
    - a drink or snack?
    - copies of all reports?
    - the agenda?
    - a pen and some paper?

2. At the beginning, does everyone agree how long the meeting should approximately last?

3. Is everyone introduced to the young person?

3a. Do they say who they are and why they are attending the meeting?

4. Is the young person given time to read through reports if she/he has not previously seen them?
    (even if she/he has seen them before some extra time may be required to jog her/his memory)

4a. Has the young person been given the option of leaving the room to read the reports in private (perhaps with a trusted adult)?

5. Is the young person given space and time to comment on different aspects of her/his life:
    - contact with family and friends?
    - school/college or work?
    - health?
    - how life is in the home?
    - relationships with social worker and linkworker/keyworker?
    - plans for the future?
    - special achievements?
    - any worries or difficult problems which she/he wants to talk about?

6. Is the young person given space to ask questions or make special requests (eg she/he may want permission to attend a school trip or visit a penfriend abroad)?

7. Do the professionals in the meeting talk about the achievements of the young person since the last review?

8. If professionals or parents say things which upset or make a young person angry, who comforts and supports her/him?

8a. If the meeting is becoming too difficult or upsetting for the young person does anyone suggest having a short break, or some people leaving the room?

Table 8: Checklist for young people's participation in reviews

After a review

---

1. Does the young person's linkworker/keyworker spend time with her/him after the review to check that:
    - she/he understands the decisions of the meeting?
    - she/he knows about the complaints procedure?

2. Does the linkworker discuss with the young person whether she/he needs any special help or information to prepare for her/his next review. If special help or information is required, is a timetable agreed?

3. Does the linkworker/keyworker make sure that the young person receives a copy of the minutes and decisions of review meeting?

4. Does the young person understand that she/he can request a review meeting *at any time?*

Encouraging participation in residential care: culture of home

The culture of a home can be determined by looking at the values of staff, interaction between young people and staff and day-to-day practices.

(i) **Do young people and staff form good relationships?**
    – What kinds of activities do young people and staff do together?
    – Do staff enjoy being with young people and vice versa?
    – Is there mutual respect between young people and staff?
    – Is there an air of competitiveness within the home and a division between staff and young people – an 'us and them' culture?

(ii) **How do staff and young people communicate?**
    – What kind of language is used to refer to young people and their families?
    – Are staff open to learning new ways of communicating (for example: sign language; making videos and audio tapes; drawing; drama)?

(iii) **How do staff manage conflict and violence?**
    – Are methods of responding to young people's behaviour fair and consistent?
    – Do staff support each other when handling conflict and violence?
    – Do staff feel able to challenge each other's practice in this area?

– Are young people clearly informed about how staff manage conflict and violence?
– Have young people participated in deciding on acceptable methods of managing behaviour (Department of Health, 1993)?

• Relationships between staff and young people develop by staff spending time with young people. Many homes actively plan – and place a high value on – time spent with young people. For example, the idea of particular 'activity nights' can be replaced by staff on each shift taking responsibility to arrange activities with young people. These activities do not have to cost lots of money;

• a culture of 'us and them' can be challenged by staff taking active measures to ensure that their home does not foster competition between staff and young people. As a reminder, the words WIN:WIN can be taped up on a wall somewhere and where there is conflict the staff and young people can aim for a solution where both sides feel they have won something;

• most staff recognise the damage and hurt that can result from them referring to young people and their families negatively. Some local authorities have taken welcome steps to encourage staff to stop using the term 'AWOL' (absent without leave) or absconder when referring to young people who run away. These terms are institutional and punitive – the only other institutions which use them are prisons and the armed forces;

• joint discussions between staff and young people can establish which language or terminology both groups find unacceptable and agreement can be reached on replacement words or phrases. Further debate can question the various meanings attributed to people and situations by the use of different words. For example, a common social work term – manipulative – is frequently used to describe circumstances where a young person is trying to take control of their life but does not have the means to do so;

• most local authorities seriously address and discourage racist language;

• many homes have booklets or guides which clearly describe to young people how staff approach conflict and violence. Most of these guides or booklets have been produced jointly by staff and young people. Many staff groups regularly meet with young people to review issues of conflict and violence, particularly bullying.

Encouraging participation in residential care: using resources effectively

Boredom among young people is a big issue in residential care. Not only is boredom not good for young people, it can also lead to all sorts of problems in the home. How many times have young people started to damage property or provoke staff because they are bored? Young people are in residential homes to be looked after. They are not there to be left to their own devices or to entertain each other, although this does not mean that they require 24 hour supervision or constant staff attention.

A lack of structure and routine can give the impression that staff have little or no expectations or interest in young people. This general apathy can have a lasting effect upon young people's education and development. During 1981/82 David Berridge spent a week living in 20 different children's homes. He found that (1985, p.115):

> *Some homes are educationally stimulating and contain numerous books, reading material and educational toys ... .Other homes are frankly dull places in which to live and do little to encourage the children's interests ... in too many homes, children return from school, bursting to recount the day's events only to find adult attention firmly focused on the chip pan and the frozen fishfingers.*

This poor and inconsistent commitment to young people's education was reflected in a recent Social Services Inspectorate and Office for Standards in Education report (1995).

Relieving boredom does not always incur financial cost. There is a whole range of activities which young people and staff can do together at very little cost. For example, a lot of young people enjoy preparing and cooking food. This is an ideal opportunity for them to get involved in the home and to learn or develop essential skills. Others will take pleasure in being the person responsible for looking after the home's car or mini-bus or a particular part of the garden. There are also many community facilities which can be used if links are made – for example youth clubs, leisure groups and membership of local libraries.

- Many homes have developed rota systems where young people take turns to cook evening meals and where all young people (if they are able) are encouraged to prepare light snacks and drinks for themselves;

- many homes actively encourage young people to join local groups and organisations. Staff can support young people's involvement by helping them with transport and showing interest and encouragement;
- many staff recognise the importance of young people participating in the running of their home and actively encourage their involvement in decision making concerned with the allocation of resources. For example, young people are encouraged to help plan holidays and special days out;
- homes can positively promote young people's education by: staff taking an active interest in young people's school work; ensuring that there are plenty of books and magazines; having money available for young people to buy newspapers, stationery, school bags and pencil cases and educational videos and computer games; and encouraging young people's individual interests and special talents or skills.

Encouraging participation in residential care: the culture of organisation

Residential services for young people have for too long been regarded as less important than other services to young people and their families. This is ironic because looking after young people is one of the most skilled and important jobs there is. Yet it is extremely rare for staff working in residential and community services to meet as colleagues, except in reviews or planning meetings, despite the fact that they belong to the same organisations and are providing services to the same young people and families.

Residential social workers are still not treated with equal status to field workers and professional rivalry exists between them. Both sets of staff complain about the others' inadequacies. Much of this is based on a misunderstanding – or lack of knowledge – about the respective positions.

How do senior managers view their responsibilities to young people in residential care? Do they resent the endless meetings with members and community groups petitioning to close homes down? Are they fed up with media attention and the spotlight of inspectors, complaints officers and children's rights officers? Is the management of residential care the area where senior managers least want to be?

Conversely, do managers enjoy the challenge and rewards of managing residential services – of which there are many? Do they take an active interest in staff and young people, in new iniatives and developments to promote young people's rights and participation? Are they pleased to have more people going into homes offering advice and support to young people?

- Some social services departments organise joint staff training for residential and field social workers;
- staff support or interest groups can be established for residential and field social workers jointly;
- some managers actively encourage residential staff to participate in departmental working groups in an effort to give them similar opportunities to field workers;
- parity of salaries is an issue which many local authorities are currently addressing;
- some senior management groups have produced written strategies for promoting young people's rights and participation within residential care;
- 28 local authorities in England and Wales have appointed children's rights and advocacy officers to promote and protect the rights of young people who are looked after;
- managers have offered support and guidance to staff about complaints procedures while also conveying the importance of them;
- social services departments can establish regular forums where they meet with young people and families who use residential services – similar to community care consultation.

Chapter ten
Conclusion

I think when you're a child, you take on the values of the people around you and if you're told you're stupid, you just go along with it and you get lumbered with not just the attitudes of your parents but the attitudes of the professionals as well. I think the attitude of the professionals was that I would never amount to anything and that's the message I got ... I always felt I was responsible for myself. I didn't feel as if anyone loved me. I felt some people liked me but – you know, if you're in an institution there's rules and regulations and I suppose things like massive big dormitories and nurses – those things aren't part of being loved by anyone.

(Terry, a disabled adult, talking about his childhood experiences of residential care in *Gone Missing?* 1995, pp17-18)

As we approach the 21st century it is essential that staff in residential homes become more sensitive and responsive to the needs and rights of young people. The first and most important reason we have residential homes is that they can provide safe, caring and nurturing environments for young people. Too often young people feel that the culture and organisation of residential care is focused upon the convenience of others – staff, managers, even their neighbours and local communities. A children's rights approach places young people at the core of our thinking and practice and constantly reminds us that they are people with feelings, views, opinions and hopes and fears just like us. Adopting a children's rights perspective symbolises two things: first that we believe young people should be treated with the same respect and regard as older people; second, that we are committed to helping young people know and claim their legal entitlements.

The wealth of research and reports depicting young people's experiences of residential and foster care generally paint a bleak picture. The overwhelming message is that young people *do not always feel listened to or valued as people.* Very rarely do these young people complain that their carers are terrible people who mean to harm them. Instead they commonly refer to administrative rules and obstacles hampering their development, or they explain how adults have failed to fully realise the consequence of their actions.

Many people complain that the idea and practice of children's rights has distracted attention away from the *real* issues in residential care – control and discipline, resources, staff cutbacks and low morale. In reality what children's rights often does is turn our minds and actions on young people and away from staff and the organisation: *young people become the most important part of residential services.* This new way of thinking – where young people are at the forefront of everything we do – means continually questioning our attitudes, practice and behaviour.

Promoting children's rights and participation is not a luxury to be introduced when budgets add up, the rotas are finished and staff sickness has been wiped out. It is important NOW. It is also not just the responsibility of residential workers – external managers especially play a key role in helping or hampering the promotion of children's rights and participation in residential services.

Children's rights can be generally categorised under three broad headings: provision; protection; and participation. Examples of rights to provision include education, health care and leisure facilities; rights to protection include child protection services and laws which prohibit child cruelty and abuse; and rights to participation include the rights of young people who are looked after to be involved in making decisions about their lives. Promoting children's rights entails all three components – a residential home which encourages young people to attend reviews but does not ask young people to choose what they have for supper, or how to decorate their bedroom, is not consistent in its approach.

While the need for good quality care and protection is uncontroversial, real challenges do arise from the third category of rights: participation. How much are young people involved in making decisions in their families, schools, local communities and in local and national politics? How much say and influence do young people who live in your residential home really have? Tackling these issues demands a different way of thinking about and relating to young people – essentially they move from being passive objects of concern (Butler Sloss 1988) to people who have ideas and views of their own. Importantly they become people who can help *us*.

If there is one message to come from this book it is this: if young people are to have a voice we older people must listen.

Bibliography

Alston, P, Parker, S and Seymour, J eds 1992 *Children, Rights and the Law*. Clarendon Press

Archard, D (1993) *Children: Rights and Childhood*. Routledge

Arnstein, S. (1969) A Ladder of Citizen Participation in the USA, *Journal of the American Institute of Planners, 35,4, 216-24*

Aries, P (1962) *Centuries of Childhood*. Jonathan Cape

Association of Black Social Workers and Probation Officers (1983) *Black Children in Care, Evidence to the House of Commons, Social Services Committee.*

Atherton, J. (1989) *Interpreting Residential Life*. Tavistock/Routledge

Bebbington, A. and Miles, J. (1989) The Background of Children who enter Local Authority Care, *British Journal of Social Work, 19, 5, 349-68*

Bennett, C. (1994) *Underclass of '94 in The Guardian Newspaper, 16 March 1994*

Beresford, P. and Croft, S. (1993) *Citizen Involvement, A Practical Guide for Change*. Macmillan

Beresford, P. and Croft, S. (1993) *Getting Involved, A Practical Manual.* Open Services project and Joseph Rowntree Foundation

Berridge, D. (1985) *Children's Homes*. Basil Blackwell

Berridge, D. (forthcoming – 1996) *Children's Homes Revisited.*

Black and In Care Steering Group (1985) *Black and In Care Conference Report*. Children's Legal Centre

Burton, J. (1993) *The Handbook of Residential Care*. Routledge

Butler, I. and Williamson, H. (1994) *Children Speak, Children, Trauma and Social Work*. Longman

Butler Sloss (1988) *Report of the Inquiry into Child Abuse in Cleveland in 1987*. HMSO

Calouste Gulbenkian Foundation (1993) *One Scandal too Many ... the Case for Comprehensive Protection in all Settings.*

Children's Rights Officers and Advocates (1995) *Directory of Children's Rights*. CROA

Children's Rights Development Unit (1994) *UK Agenda for Children.* CRDU

The Children's Society (1993) *The Case against Locking up More Children.*

Cohen, S. (1972) *Folk Devils and Moral Panics, the Creation of the Mods and Rockers.* Basil Blackwell

Collins, S. and Stein, M. (1989) *in* Rojek, C., Peacock, G., and Collins, S. eds. (1989) *op cit*

Crompton, M. (1980) *Respecting Children: Social Work with Young People.* Edward Arnold

Dalrymple, J. and Hough, J. (1995) *Having A Voice, An Exploration of Children's Rights and Advocacy.* Venture Press

Dartington Social Research Unit in conjunction with Support Force for Children's Residential Care (1995) *Matching Needs with Services, The Audit and Planning of Provision for Children Looked After by Local Authorities.* Dartington Social Research Unit

Department of Health (1988) *A Guide for Social Workers Undertaking a Comprehensive Assessment.* HMSO

Department of Health (1991) *The Children Act Guidance and Regulations Volume 4 Residential Care.* HMSO

Department of Health (1993) *Permissible Forms of Control in Children's Residential Care.*

Department of Health (1994) *Guidelines on Smoking and Alcohol Consumption in Residential Child Care Establishments.*

Department of Health (1996) *Children Looked After by Local Authorities year ending 31 March 1995, England.* Statistical Bulletin.

Department of Health and Social Security (1986) *Social Work Decisions in Child Care, Recent Research Findings and their Implications.* HMSO

Department of Health Social Services Inspectorate and Office for Standards in Education (1995) *The Education of Children who are Looked After by Local Authorities.*

Department of Health Social Services Inspectorate (1994) *Standards for Residential Child Care Services.* HMSO

The Dolphin Project (1993) *Answering Back, Report by Young People being Looked After on the Children Act 1989.* University of Southampton

Ellis, S. and Franklin, A. *in* Franklin, R. *ed* (1995) *The Handbook of Children's Rights, Comparative Policy and Practice.* Routledge

Fletcher, B. (1993) *Not Just a Name, the Views of Young People in Foster and Residential Care.* National Consumer Council

Franklin, R. *ed* (1995) *The Handbook of Children's Rights.* Routledge

Franklin, R. ed (1986) *The Rights of Children.* Basil Blackwell

Freeman, MDA (1983) *The Rights and Wrongs of Children.* Frances Pinter

Frost, N and Stein, M (1989) *The Politics of Child Welfare, Inequality, Power and Change.* Harvester Wheatsheaf

Gardner, R. (1987) *Who Says? Coice and Control in Care.* National Children's Bureau

Harris, R. and Timms, N. (1993) *Secure Accommodation in Child Care, between Hospital and Prison or thereabouts.* Routledge

Hart, R. (1992) *Children's Participation, from Tokenism to Citizenship* UNICEF

Heartfield, J. (1993) Why Children's Rights are Wrong, *Living Marxism, October 1993*

Heywood, J.S. (1979) *Children in Care, the Development of the Service for the Deprived Child.* Routledge and Kegan Paul

Hodgkin, R. (1995) *Safe to Let Out? The Current and Future Use of Secure Accommodation for Children and Young People.* National Children's Bureau

Hodgkin, R. (1994) Government Plans for Travellers, *Children and Society, 8, 3, 274-278*

Holt, J (1974) *Escape from Childhood.* Penguin

Hoyles, M (1985) *The Politics of Childhood.* Journeyman

Howe (1992) *The Quality of Care, Report of the Residential Staffs Inquiry.* Local Government Management Board

Jones, A and others (1992) *A Home for Home: the Experiences of Black Residential Projects as a Focus of Good Practice.* National Institute for Social Work

Kahan, B. (1994) *Growing Up in Groups.* HMSO

Kahan, B. (1979) *Growing Up in Care, Ten People Talking.* Basil Blackwell

Kirkwood, A. (1993) *The Leicestershire Inquiry.* Leicestershire County Council

Hampshire County Council (1993) *Listening to Children.* Hampshire County Council Social Services Department

Levy, A. and Kahan, B. (1991) *The Pindown Experience and the Protection of Children.* Staffordshire County Council

Macdonald, S (1991) *All Equal Under the Act.* Race Equality Unit

Milham, S., Bullock, R., Hosie, K. and Haak, M. (1986) *Lost in Care, The Problems of Maintaining Links between Children in Care and their Families.* Gower

Miller, A. (1987) *The Drama of Being a Child.* Virago

Morris, J. (1995) *Gone Missing? A Research and Policy Review of Disabled Children Living Away from their Families.* Who Cares? Trust

Morris, S. and Wheatley, H. (1994) *Time to Listen, the Experiences of Children in Residential and Foster Care.* Childline

Newell, P. (1989) *Children are People too: the Case Against Physical Punishment.* Bedford Square Press

Nottinghamshire County Council (1992) *As if They Were Our Own. Raising the Quality of Residential Child Care in Nottinghamshire: the Report of the Chief Executive's Working Party*

O'Neill, T. (1981) *A Place called Hope.* Basil Blackwell

OPCS (1994) *1991 Census, Children and Young Adults, Great Britain, Volume One* HMSO

Packman, J. (1981) *The Child's Generation.* Basil Blackwell

Page, R. and Clark, G.A. *ed* (1977) *Who Cares?* National Children's Bureau

Parker, R. and others *eds* (1991) *Looking After Children. Assessing Outcomes in Child Care. The Report of an Independent Working Party established by the Department of Health.* HMSO

Parker, R. (1990) *Away from Home, A History of Child Care.* Barnardo's

Patel, S. (1995) *Directory of In-Care and After-Care Groups in the United Kingdom.* Save the Children

Pinchbeck, I and Hewitt, M (1973) *Children in English Society (Volumes 1 and 2).* Routledge and Kegan Paul

Riddell, M (1996) *The Cornflake Kid.* Partnership Publications

Rogers, R. and Rogers, W. (1992) *Stories of Childhood, Shifting Agendas of Child Concern.* Harvester Wheatsheaf

Rojek, C., Peacock, G. and Collins, S. *eds.* (1989) *The Haunt of Misery, Critical Essays in Social Work and Helping.* Routledge

Rowe, J., Hundleby, M. and Garnett, L. (1989) *Child Care Now, a Survey of Placement Patterns.* British Agencies for Adoption and Fostering

Russell, P. (1994) *in* Morris, J. (1995) *ibid.*

Support Force for Children's Residential Care (1995a) *Code of Practice for the Employment of Residential Child Care Workers.* Department of Health

Support Force for Children's Residential Care (1995b) *Good Care Matters, Ways of Enhancing Good Practice in Residential Child Care.* Department of Health

Support Force for Children's Residential Care (1995c) *Staff Supervision in Children's Homes.* Department of Health

Utting, W. (1991) *Children in the Public Care.* HMSO

Walton, R. (1979) in Crompton (1980) *ibid.*

Warner, N. (1992) *Choosing with Care, the Report of the Committee of Inquiry into the Selection, Development and Management of Staff in Children's Homes.* HMSO

Wheal, A and Buchanan, A (1994) *Answers, a Handbook for Residential and Foster Carers of Young People aged 11-18 years.* Longman

Wheal, A. and Sinclair, R. (1995) *It's YOUR Meeting, a Guide to Help Young People get the Most from their Review.* National Children's Bureau

Who Cares? Magazine 1994 (issue 29)

Willow, C. (1995) *A Word in Edgeways.* Unpublished report – available from National Children's Bureau

Wringe, CA (1981) *Children's Rights, a Philosophical Study.* Routledge and Kegan Paul

Youth Council for Northern Ireland (1993) *Participation, Youth Work Curriculum*

Useful contacts – children's rights organisations

Advice, Advocacy and Representation Services for Children (ASC)
1 Sickle Street
Manchester M60 2AA
0800 616101

Black and In Care
300 Moss Lane East
Moss Side
Manchester M14 4LZ
0161 226 9122

Childline (for children and young people in residential and foster care)
Freepost 1111
London N1 0BR
0800 884 444 (6-10pm)

Children's Legal Centre
University of Essex
Wivenhoe Park
Colchester
Essex CO4 3SQ
0120 687 3820 (2-5 pm)

Children's Rights Office
235 Shaftesbury Avenue
London WC2H 8EL
0171 240 4449

Children's Rights Officers and Advocates (CROA)
c/o Wales Advocacy Unit
14 Cathedral Road
Cardiff CF1 9LJ
0122 266 8956

End Physical Punishment of Children (EPOCH)
77 Holloway Road
London N7 8JZ
0171 700 0627

Voice for the Child in Care
Unit 4, Pride Court
80-82 White Lion Street
London N1 9PF
0171 833 5792

Who Cares? Trust
Kemp House
152-160 City Road
London EC1V 2NP
0171 251 3117
Telephone Linkline for young people in residential and foster care:
0500 564570 (Mon, Wed, Thurs, 3.30-6.30pm)

Useful contacts
– young people's organisations

Article 12 *(an organisation of young people which aims to implement Article 12 of the UN Convention)*
National Children's Bureau
8 Wakley Street
London
EC1V 7QE
0171 843 6026

Children's Express *(a news agency producing news and comments by people aged eight to 18)*
3-11 Pine Street
London
EC1 0JH
0171 833 2577

Underground Power *(an organisation of young people campaigning for rights for all young people)*
9 Osmaston Road
Birkenhead
Merseyside
L42 8PY

Voices from Care *(an organisation of young people who are, or who have been, looked after)*
254 Cowbridge Road East
Cardiff
CF5 1GZ
0122 239 8214

Who Cares? Scotland *(an organisation of young people who are, or have been, looked after)*
Block 4
Unit C3
Templeton Business Centre
Templeton Street
Glasgow
G40 1DA
0141 554 4452

Young People First *(a speaking up organisation run by and for young people with learning difficulties)*
Instrument House
207–215 Kings Cross Road
London
WC1X 9DB

Index

Entries are arranged in letter-by-letter order (hyphens and spaces between words are ignored).